ISBN 0-8373-1345-7

C-1345   CAREER EXAMINATION SERIES

This is your
PASSBOOK® for...

Library Assistant

Test Preparation Study Guide

Questions & Answers

NLC

NATIONAL LEARNING CORPORATION

PASSBOOK®

NOTICE

This book is *SOLELY* intended for, is sold *ONLY* to, and its use is *RESTRICTED* to *individual,* bona fide applicants or candidates who qualify by virtue of having seriously filed applications for appropriate license, certificate, professional and/or promotional advancement, higher school matriculation, scholarship, or other legitimate requirements of educational and/or governmental authorities.

This book is *NOT* intended for use, class instruction, tutoring, training, duplication, copying, reprinting, excerption, or adaptation, etc., by:

(1) Other Publishers

(2) Proprietors and/or Instructors of "Coaching" and/or Preparatory Courses

(3) Personnel and/or Training Divisions of commercial, industrial, and governmental organizations

(4) Schools, colleges, or universities and/or their departments and staffs, including teachers and other personnel

(5) Testing Agencies or Bureaus

(6) Study groups which seek by the purchase of a single volume to copy and/or duplicate and/or adapt this material for use by the group as a whole without having purchased individual volumes for each of the members of the group

(7) Et al.

Such persons would be in violation of appropriate Federal and State statutes.

PROVISION OF LICENSING AGREEMENTS. — Recognized educational commercial, industrial, and governmental institutions and organizations, and others legitimately engaged in educational pursuits, including training, testing, and measurement activities, may address a request for a licensing agreement to the copyright owners, who will determine whether, and under what conditions, including fees and charges, the materials in this book may be used by them. In other words, a licensing facility *exists* for the legitimate use of the material in this book on other than an individual basis. However, it is asseverated and affirmed here that the materials in this book *CANNOT* be used without the receipt of the express permission of such a licensing agreement from the Publishers.

NATIONAL LEARNING CORPORATION
212 Michael Drive
Syosset, New York 11791

Inquiries re licensing agreements should be addressed to:
The President
National Learning Corporation
212 Michael Drive
Syosset, New York 11791

PASSBOOK SERIES®

THE *PASSBOOK SERIES®* has been created to prepare applicants and candidates for the ultimate academic battlefield – the examination room.

At some time in our lives, each and every one of us may be required to take an examination – for validation, matriculation, admission, qualification, registration, certification, or licensure.

Based on the assumption that every applicant or candidate has met the basic formal educational standards, has taken the required number of courses, and read the necessary texts, the *PASSBOOK SERIES®* furnishes the one special preparation which may assure passing with confidence, instead of failing with insecurity. Examination questions – together with answers – are furnished as the basic vehicle for study so that the mysteries of the examination and its compounding difficulties may be eliminated or diminished by a sure method.

This book is meant to help you pass your examination provided that you qualify and are serious in your objective.

The entire field is reviewed through the huge store of content information which is succinctly presented through a provocative and challenging approach – the question-and-answer method.

A climate of success is established by furnishing the correct answers at the end of each test.

You soon learn to recognize types of questions, forms of questions, and patterns of questioning. You may even begin to anticipate expected outcomes.

You perceive that many questions are repeated or adapted so that you can gain acute insights, which may enable you to score many sure points.

You learn how to confront new questions, or types of questions, and to attack them confidently and work out the correct answers.

You note objectives and emphases, and recognize pitfalls and dangers, so that you may make positive educational adjustments.

Moreover, you are kept fully informed in relation to new concepts, methods, practices, and directions in the field.

You discover that you are actually taking the examination all the time: you are preparing for the examination by "taking" an examination, not by reading extraneous and/or supererogatory textbooks.

In short, this PASSBOOK®, used directedly, should be an important factor in helping you to pass your test.

LIBRARY ASSISTANT

DUTIES

Assists professional librarians in the performance of all library functions. Explains to library-users the card catalog and the arrangement of books on shelves. Performs rudimentary cataloging, classification, and reference services. May accept responsibility for a subject area and recommend titles for purchase and discard. Prepares drafts of memoranda and correspondence. Supervises subordinate personnel as needed.

SCOPE OF THE WRITTEN TEST

The written test will be designed to cover knowledges, skills, and/or abilities in the following areas:
1. Preparation of written material;
2. Understanding and interpreting written material;
3. Vocabulary;
4. Verbal Analogies; and
5. Understanding and interpreting tabular materials.

HOW TO TAKE A TEST

I. YOU MUST PASS AN EXAMINATION

A. WHAT EVERY CANDIDATE SHOULD KNOW

Examination applicants often ask us for help in preparing for the written test. What can I study in advance? What kinds of questions will be asked? How will the test be given? How will the papers be graded?

As an applicant for a civil service examination, you may be wondering about some of these things. Our purpose here is to suggest effective methods of advance study and to describe civil service examinations.

Your chances for success on this examination can be increased if you know how to prepare. Those "pre-examination jitters" can be reduced if you know what to expect. You can even experience an adventure in good citizenship if you know why civil service exams are given.

B. WHY ARE CIVIL SERVICE EXAMINATIONS GIVEN?

Civil service examinations are important to you in two ways. As a citizen, you want public jobs filled by employees who know how to do their work. As a job seeker, you want a fair chance to compete for that job on an equal footing with other candidates. The best-known means of accomplishing this two-fold goal is the competitive examination.

Exams are widely publicized throughout the nation. They may be administered for jobs in federal, state, city, municipal, town or village governments or agencies.

Any citizen may apply, with some limitations, such as the age or residence of applicants. Your experience and education may be reviewed to see whether you meet the requirements for the particular examination. When these requirements exist, they are reasonable and applied consistently to all applicants. Thus, a competitive examination may cause you some uneasiness now, but it is your privilege and safeguard.

C. HOW ARE CIVIL SERVICE EXAMS DEVELOPED?

Examinations are carefully written by trained technicians who are specialists in the field known as "psychological measurement," in consultation with recognized authorities in the field of work that the test will cover. These experts recommend the subject matter areas or skills to be tested; only those knowledges or skills important to your success on the job are included. The most reliable books and source materials available are used as references. Together, the experts and technicians judge the difficulty level of the questions.

Test technicians know how to phrase questions so that the problem is clearly stated. Their ethics do not permit "trick" or "catch" questions. Questions may have been tried out on sample groups, or subjected to statistical analysis, to determine their usefulness.

Written tests are often used in combination with performance tests, ratings of training and experience, and oral interviews. All of these measures combine to form the best-known means of finding the right person for the right job.

II. HOW TO PASS THE WRITTEN TEST

A. NATURE OF THE EXAMINATION

To prepare intelligently for civil service examinations, you should know how they differ from school examinations you have taken. In school you were assigned certain definite pages to read or subjects to cover. The examination questions were quite detailed and usually emphasized memory. Civil service exams, on the other hand, try to discover your present ability to perform the duties of a position, plus your potentiality to learn these duties. In other words, a civil service exam attempts to predict how successful you will be. Questions cover such a broad area that they cannot be as minute and detailed as school exam questions.

In the public service similar kinds of work, or positions, are grouped together in one "class." This process is known as *position-classification*. All the positions in a class are paid according to the salary range for that class. One class title covers all of these positions, and they are all tested by the same examination.

B. FOUR BASIC STEPS

1) Study the announcement

How, then, can you know what subjects to study? Our best answer is: "Learn as much as possible about the class of positions for which you've applied." The exam will test the knowledge, skills and abilities needed to do the work.

Your most valuable source of information about the position you want is the official exam announcement. This announcement lists the training and experience qualifications. Check these standards and apply only if you come reasonably close to meeting them.

The brief description of the position in the examination announcement offers some clues to the subjects which will be tested. Think about the job itself. Review the duties in your mind. Can you perform them, or are there some in which you are rusty? Fill in the blank spots in your preparation.

Many jurisdictions preview the written test in the exam announcement by including a section called "Knowledge and Abilities Required," "Scope of the Examination," or some similar heading. Here you will find out specifically what fields will be tested.

2) Review your own background

Once you learn in general what the position is all about, and what you need to know to do the work, ask yourself which subjects you already know fairly well and which need improvement. You may wonder whether to concentrate on improving your strong areas or on building some background in your fields of weakness. When the announcement has specified "some knowledge" or "considerable knowledge," or has used adjectives like "beginning principles of…" or "advanced … methods," you can get a clue as to the number and difficulty of questions to be asked in any given field. More questions, and hence broader coverage, would be included for those subjects which are more important in the work. Now weigh your strengths and weaknesses against the job requirements and prepare accordingly.

3) Determine the level of the position

Another way to tell how intensively you should prepare is to understand the level of the job for which you are applying. Is it the entering level? In other words, is this the position in which beginners in a field of work are hired? Or is it an intermediate or advanced level? Sometimes this is indicated by such words as "Junior" or "Senior" in the class title. Other jurisdictions use Roman numerals to designate the level – Clerk I, Clerk II, for example. The word "Supervisor" sometimes appears in the title. If the level is not indicated by the title, check the description of duties. Will you be working under very close supervision, or will you have responsibility for independent decisions in this work?

4) Choose appropriate study materials

Now that you know the subjects to be examined and the relative amount of each subject to be covered, you can choose suitable study materials. For beginning level jobs, or even advanced ones, if you have a pronounced weakness in some aspect of your training, read a modern, standard textbook in that field. Be sure it is up to date and has general coverage. Such books are normally available at your library, and the librarian will be glad to help you locate one. For entry-level positions, questions of appropriate difficulty are chosen – neither highly advanced questions, nor those too simple. Such questions require careful thought but not advanced training.

If the position for which you are applying is technical or advanced, you will read more advanced, specialized material. If you are already familiar with the basic principles of your field, elementary textbooks would waste your time. Concentrate on advanced textbooks and technical periodicals. Think through the concepts and review difficult problems in your field.

These are all general sources. You can get more ideas on your own initiative, following these leads. For example, training manuals and publications of the government agency which employs workers in your field can be useful, particularly for technical and professional positions. A letter or visit to the government department involved may result in more specific study suggestions, and certainly will provide you with a more definite idea of the exact nature of the position you are seeking.

III. KINDS OF TESTS

Tests are used for purposes other than measuring knowledge and ability to perform specified duties. For some positions, it is equally important to test ability to make adjustments to new situations or to profit from training. In others, basic mental abilities not dependent on information are essential. Questions which test these things may not appear as pertinent to the duties of the position as those which test for knowledge and information. Yet they are often highly important parts of a fair examination. For very general questions, it is almost impossible to help you direct your study efforts. What we can do is to point out some of the more common of these general abilities needed in public service positions and describe some typical questions.

1) General information

Broad, general information has been found useful for predicting job success in some kinds of work. This is tested in a variety of ways, from vocabulary lists to questions about current events. Basic background in some field of work, such as sociology or economics, may be sampled in a group of questions. Often these are principles which have become familiar to most persons through exposure rather than through formal training. It is difficult to advise you how to study for these questions; being alert to the world around you is our best suggestion.

2) Verbal ability

An example of an ability needed in many positions is verbal or language ability. Verbal ability is, in brief, the ability to use and understand words. Vocabulary and grammar tests are typical measures of this ability. Reading comprehension or paragraph interpretation questions are common in many kinds of civil service tests. You are given a paragraph of written material and asked to find its central meaning.

3) Numerical ability

Number skills can be tested by the familiar arithmetic problem, by checking paired lists of numbers to see which are alike and which are different, or by interpreting charts and graphs. In the latter test, a graph may be printed in the test booklet which you are asked to use as the basis for answering questions.

4) Observation

A popular test for law-enforcement positions is the observation test. A picture is shown to you for several minutes, then taken away. Questions about the picture test your ability to observe both details and larger elements.

5) Following directions

In many positions in the public service, the employee must be able to carry out written instructions dependably and accurately. You may be given a chart with several columns, each column listing a variety of information. The questions require you to carry out directions involving the information given in the chart.

6) Skills and aptitudes

Performance tests effectively measure some manual skills and aptitudes. When the skill is one in which you are trained, such as typing or shorthand, you can practice. These tests are often very much like those given in business school or high school courses. For many of the other skills and aptitudes, however, no short-time preparation can be made. Skills and abilities natural to you or that you have developed throughout your lifetime are being tested.

Many of the general questions just described provide all the data needed to answer the questions and ask you to use your reasoning ability to find the answers. Your best preparation for these tests, as well as for tests of facts and ideas, is to be at your physical and mental best. You, no doubt, have your own methods of getting into an exam-taking mood and keeping "in shape." The next section lists some ideas on this subject.

IV. KINDS OF QUESTIONS

Only rarely is the "essay" question, which you answer in narrative form, used in civil service tests. Civil service tests are usually of the short-answer type. Full instructions for answering these questions will be given to you at the examination. But in case this is your first experience with short-answer questions and separate answer sheets, here is what you need to know:

1) Multiple-choice Questions

Most popular of the short-answer questions is the "multiple choice" or "best answer" question. It can be used, for example, to test for factual knowledge, ability to solve problems or judgment in meeting situations found at work.

A multiple-choice question is normally one of three types—

- It can begin with an incomplete statement followed by several possible endings. You are to find the one ending which *best* completes the statement, although some of the others may not be entirely wrong.
- It can also be a complete statement in the form of a question which is answered by choosing one of the statements listed.
- It can be in the form of a problem – again you select the best answer.

Here is an example of a multiple-choice question with a discussion which should give you some clues as to the method for choosing the right answer:

When an employee has a complaint about his assignment, the action which will *best* help him overcome his difficulty is to
A. discuss his difficulty with his coworkers
B. take the problem to the head of the organization
C. take the problem to the person who gave him the assignment
D. say nothing to anyone about his complaint

In answering this question, you should study each of the choices to find which is best. Consider choice "A" – Certainly an employee may discuss his complaint with fellow employees, but no change or improvement can result, and the complaint remains unresolved. Choice "B" is a poor choice since the head of the organization probably does not know what assignment you have been given, and taking your problem to him is known as "going over the head" of the supervisor. The supervisor, or person who made the assignment, is the person who can clarify it or correct any injustice. Choice "C" is, therefore, correct. To say nothing, as in choice "D," is unwise. Supervisors have and interest in knowing the problems employees are facing, and the employee is seeking a solution to his problem.

2) True/False Questions

The "true/false" or "right/wrong" form of question is sometimes used. Here a complete statement is given. Your job is to decide whether the statement is right or wrong.

SAMPLE: A person-to-person long-distance telephone call costs less than a station-to-station call to the same city.

This statement is wrong, or false, since person-to-person calls are more expensive.

This is not a complete list of all possible question forms, although most of the others are variations of these common types. You will always get complete directions for answering questions. Be sure you understand *how* to mark your answers – ask questions until you do.

V. RECORDING YOUR ANSWERS

For an examination with very few applicants, you may be told to record your answers in the test booklet itself. Separate answer sheets are much more common. If this separate answer sheet is to be scored by machine – and this is often the case – it is highly important that you mark your answers correctly in order to get credit.

An electric scoring machine is often used in civil service offices because of the speed with which papers can be scored. Machine-scored answer sheets must be marked with a pencil, which will be given to you. This pencil has a high graphite content which responds to the electric scoring machine. As a matter of fact, stray dots may register as answers, so do not let your pencil rest on the answer sheet while you are pondering the correct answer. Also, if your pencil lead breaks or is otherwise defective, ask for another.

Since the answer sheet will be dropped in a slot in the scoring machine, be careful not to bend the corners or get the paper crumpled.

The answer sheet normally has five vertical columns of numbers, with 30 numbers to a column. These numbers correspond to the question numbers in your test booklet. After each number, going across the page are four or five pairs of dotted lines. These short dotted lines have small letters or numbers above them. The first two pairs may also have a "T" or "F" above the letters. This indicates that the first two pairs only are to be used if the questions are of the true-false type. If the questions are multiple choice, disregard the "T" and "F" and pay attention only to the small letters or numbers.

Answer your questions in the manner of the sample that follows:

32. The largest city in the United States is
    A. Washington, D.C.
    B. New York City
    C. Chicago
    D. Detroit
    E. San Francisco

1) Choose the answer you think is best. (New York City is the largest, so "B" is correct.)
2) Find the row of dotted lines numbered the same as the question you are answering. (Find row number 32)
3) Find the pair of dotted lines corresponding to the answer. (Find the pair of lines under the mark "B.")
4) Make a solid black mark between the dotted lines.

VI. BEFORE THE TEST

Common sense will help you find procedures to follow to get ready for an examination. Too many of us, however, overlook these sensible measures. Indeed, nervousness and fatigue have been found to be the most serious reasons why applicants fail to do their best on civil service tests. Here is a list of reminders:

- Begin your preparation early – Don't wait until the last minute to go scurrying around for books and materials or to find out what the position is all about.
- Prepare continuously – An hour a night for a week is better than an all-night cram session. This has been definitely established. What is more, a night a

week for a month will return better dividends than crowding your study into a shorter period of time.

- Locate the place of the exam – You have been sent a notice telling you when and where to report for the examination. If the location is in a different town or otherwise unfamiliar to you, it would be well to inquire the best route and learn something about the building.
- Relax the night before the test – Allow your mind to rest. Do not study at all that night. Plan some mild recreation or diversion; then go to bed early and get a good night's sleep.
- Get up early enough to make a leisurely trip to the place for the test – This way unforeseen events, traffic snarls, unfamiliar buildings, etc. will not upset you.
- Dress comfortably – A written test is not a fashion show. You will be known by number and not by name, so wear something comfortable.
- Leave excess paraphernalia at home – Shopping bags and odd bundles will get in your way. You need bring only the items mentioned in the official notice you received; usually everything you need is provided. Do not bring reference books to the exam. They will only confuse those last minutes and be taken away from you when in the test room.
- Arrive somewhat ahead of time – If because of transportation schedules you must get there very early, bring a newspaper or magazine to take your mind off yourself while waiting.
- Locate the examination room – When you have found the proper room, you will be directed to the seat or part of the room where you will sit. Sometimes you are given a sheet of instructions to read while you are waiting. Do not fill out any forms until you are told to do so; just read them and be prepared.
- Relax and prepare to listen to the instructions
- If you have any physical problem that may keep you from doing your best, be sure to tell the test administrator. If you are sick or in poor health, you really cannot do your best on the exam. You can come back and take the test some other time.

VII. AT THE TEST

The day of the test is here and you have the test booklet in your hand. The temptation to get going is very strong. Caution! There is more to success than knowing the right answers. You must know how to identify your papers and understand variations in the type of short-answer question used in this particular examination. Follow these suggestions for maximum results from your efforts:

1) Cooperate with the monitor
The test administrator has a duty to create a situation in which you can be as much at ease as possible. He will give instructions, tell you when to begin, check to see that you are marking your answer sheet correctly, and so on. He is not there to guard you, although he will see that your competitors do not take unfair advantage. He wants to help you do your best.

2) Listen to all instructions
Don't jump the gun! Wait until you understand all directions. In most civil service tests you get more time than you need to answer the questions. So don't be in a hurry.

Read each word of instructions until you clearly understand the meaning. Study the examples, listen to all announcements and follow directions. Ask questions if you do not understand what to do.

3) Identify your papers

Civil service exams are usually identified by number only. You will be assigned a number; you must not put your name on your test papers. Be sure to copy your number correctly. Since more than one exam may be given, copy your exact examination title.

4) Plan your time

Unless you are told that a test is a "speed" or "rate of work" test, speed itself is usually not important. Time enough to answer all the questions will be provided, but this does not mean that you have all day. An overall time limit has been set. Divide the total time (in minutes) by the number of questions to determine the approximate time you have for each question.

5) Do not linger over difficult questions

If you come across a difficult question, mark it with a paper clip (useful to have along) and come back to it when you have been through the booklet. One caution if you do this – be sure to skip a number on your answer sheet as well. Check often to be sure that you have not lost your place and that you are marking in the row numbered the same as the question you are answering.

6) Read the questions

Be sure you know what the question asks! Many capable people are unsuccessful because they failed to *read* the questions correctly.

7) Answer all questions

Unless you have been instructed that a penalty will be deducted for incorrect answers, it is better to guess than to omit a question.

8) Speed tests

It is often better NOT to guess on speed tests. It has been found that on timed tests people are tempted to spend the last few seconds before time is called in marking answers at random – without even reading them – in the hope of picking up a few extra points. To discourage this practice, the instructions may warn you that your score will be "corrected" for guessing. That is, a penalty will be applied. The incorrect answers will be deducted from the correct ones, or some other penalty formula will be used.

9) Review your answers

If you finish before time is called, go back to the questions you guessed or omitted to give them further thought. Review other answers if you have time.

10) Return your test materials

If you are ready to leave before others have finished or time is called, take ALL your materials to the monitor and leave quietly. Never take any test material with you. The monitor can discover whose papers are not complete, and taking a test booklet may be grounds for disqualification.

VIII. EXAMINATION TECHNIQUES

1) Read the general instructions carefully. These are usually printed on the first page of the exam booklet. As a rule, these instructions refer to the timing of the examination; the fact that you should not start work until the signal and must stop work at a signal, etc. If there are any *special* instructions, such as a choice of questions to be answered, make sure that you note this instruction carefully.

2) When you are ready to start work on the examination, that is as soon as the signal has been given, read the instructions to each question booklet, underline any key words or phrases, such as *least, best, outline, describe* and the like. In this way you will tend to answer as requested rather than discover on reviewing your paper that you *listed without describing*, that you selected the *worst* choice rather than the *best* choice, etc.

3) If the examination is of the objective or multiple-choice type – that is, each question will also give a series of possible answers: A, B, C or D, and you are called upon to select the best answer and write the letter next to that answer on your answer paper – it is advisable to start answering each question in turn. There may be anywhere from 50 to 100 such questions in the three or four hours allotted and you can see how much time would be taken if you read through all the questions before beginning to answer any. Furthermore, if you come across a question or group of questions which you know would be difficult to answer, it would undoubtedly affect your handling of all the other questions.

4) If the examination is of the essay type and contains but a few questions, it is a moot point as to whether you should read all the questions before starting to answer any one. Of course, if you are given a choice – say five out of seven and the like – then it is essential to read all the questions so you can eliminate the two that are most difficult. If, however, you are asked to answer all the questions, there may be danger in trying to answer the easiest one first because you may find that you will spend too much time on it. The best technique is to answer the first question, then proceed to the second, etc.

5) Time your answers. Before the exam begins, write down the time it started, then add the time allowed for the examination and write down the time it must be completed, then divide the time available somewhat as follows:
   - If 3-1/2 hours are allowed, that would be 210 minutes. If you have 80 objective-type questions, that would be an average of 2-1/2 minutes per question. Allow yourself no more than 2 minutes per question, or a total of 160 minutes, which will permit about 50 minutes to review.
   - If for the time allotment of 210 minutes there are 7 essay questions to answer, that would average about 30 minutes a question. Give yourself only 25 minutes per question so that you have about 35 minutes to review.

6) The most important instruction is to *read each question* and make sure you know what is wanted. The second most important instruction is to *time yourself properly* so that you answer every question. The third most

important instruction is to *answer every question*. Guess if you have to but include something for each question. Remember that you will receive no credit for a blank and will probably receive some credit if you write something in answer to an essay question. If you guess a letter – say "B" for a multiple-choice question – you may have guessed right. If you leave a blank as an answer to a multiple-choice question, the examiners may respect your feelings but it will not add a point to your score. Some exams may penalize you for wrong answers, so in such cases *only*, you may not want to guess unless you have some basis for your answer.

7) Suggestions
   a. Objective-type questions
      1. Examine the question booklet for proper sequence of pages and questions
      2. Read all instructions carefully
      3. Skip any question which seems too difficult; return to it after all other questions have been answered
      4. Apportion your time properly; do not spend too much time on any single question or group of questions
      5. Note and underline key words – *all, most, fewest, least, best, worst, same, opposite,* etc.
      6. Pay particular attention to negatives
      7. Note unusual option, e.g., unduly long, short, complex, different or similar in content to the body of the question
      8. Observe the use of "hedging" words – *probably, may, most likely,* etc.
      9. Make sure that your answer is put next to the same number as the question
      10. Do not second-guess unless you have good reason to believe the second answer is definitely more correct
      11. Cross out original answer if you decide another answer is more accurate; do not erase until you are ready to hand your paper in
      12. Answer all questions; guess unless instructed otherwise
      13. Leave time for review

   b. Essay questions
      1. Read each question carefully
      2. Determine exactly what is wanted. Underline key words or phrases.
      3. Decide on outline or paragraph answer
      4. Include many different points and elements unless asked to develop any one or two points or elements
      5. Show impartiality by giving pros and cons unless directed to select one side only
      6. Make and write down any assumptions you find necessary to answer the questions
      7. Watch your English, grammar, punctuation and choice of words
      8. Time your answers; don't crowd material

8) Answering the essay question

Most essay questions can be answered by framing the specific response around several key words or ideas. Here are a few such key words or ideas:

M's: manpower, materials, methods, money, management

P's: purpose, program, policy, plan, procedure, practice, problems, pitfalls, personnel, public relations

    a. Six basic steps in handling problems:
1. Preliminary plan and background development
2. Collect information, data and facts
3. Analyze and interpret information, data and facts
4. Analyze and develop solutions as well as make recommendations
5. Prepare report and sell recommendations
6. Install recommendations and follow up effectiveness

    b. Pitfalls to avoid
1. *Taking things for granted* – A statement of the situation does not necessarily imply that each of the elements is necessarily true; for example, a complaint may be invalid and biased so that all that can be taken for granted is that a complaint has been registered
2. *Considering only one side of a situation* – Wherever possible, indicate several alternatives and then point out the reasons you selected the best one
3. *Failing to indicate follow up* – Whenever your answer indicates action on your part, make certain that you will take proper follow-up action to see how successful your recommendations, procedures or actions turn out to be
4. *Taking too long in answering any single question* – Remember to time your answers properly

IX. AFTER THE TEST

Scoring procedures differ in detail among civil service jurisdictions although the general principles are the same. Whether the papers are hand-scored or graded by machine we have described, they are nearly always graded by number. That is, the person who marks the paper knows only the number – never the name – of the applicant. Not until all the papers have been graded will they be matched with names. If other tests, such as training and experience or oral interview ratings have been given, scores will be combined. Different parts of the examination usually have different weights. For example, the written test might count 60 percent of the final grade, and a rating of training and experience 40 percent. In many jurisdictions, veterans will have a certain number of points added to their grades.

After the final grade has been determined, the names are placed in grade order and an eligible list is established. There are various methods for resolving ties between those who get the same final grade – probably the most common is to place first the name of the person whose application was received first. Job offers are made from the eligible list in the order the names appear on it. You will be notified of your grade and your rank as soon as all these computations have been made. This will be done as rapidly as possible.

People who are found to meet the requirements in the announcement are called "eligibles." Their names are put on a list of eligible candidates. An eligible's chances of getting a job depend on how high he stands on this list and how fast agencies are filling jobs from the list.

When a job is to be filled from a list of eligibles, the agency asks for the names of people on the list of eligibles for that job. When the civil service commission receives this request, it sends to the agency the names of the three people highest on this list. Or, if the job to be filled has specialized requirements, the office sends the agency the names of the top three persons who meet these requirements from the general list.

The appointing officer makes a choice from among the three people whose names were sent to him. If the selected person accepts the appointment, the names of the others are put back on the list to be considered for future openings.

That is the rule in hiring from all kinds of eligible lists, whether they are for typist, carpenter, chemist, or something else. For every vacancy, the appointing officer has his choice of any one of the top three eligibles on the list. This explains why the person whose name is on top of the list sometimes does not get an appointment when some of the persons lower on the list do. If the appointing officer chooses the second or third eligible, the No. 1 eligible does not get a job at once, but stays on the list until he is appointed or the list is terminated.

X. HOW TO PASS THE INTERVIEW TEST

The examination for which you applied requires an oral interview test. You have already taken the written test and you are now being called for the interview test – the final part of the formal examination.

You may think that it is not possible to prepare for an interview test and that there are no procedures to follow during an interview. Our purpose is to point out some things you can do in advance that will help you and some good rules to follow and pitfalls to avoid while you are being interviewed.

What is an interview supposed to test?

The written examination is designed to test the technical knowledge and competence of the candidate; the oral is designed to evaluate intangible qualities, not readily measured otherwise, and to establish a list showing the relative fitness of each candidate – as measured against his competitors – for the position sought. Scoring is not on the basis of "right" and "wrong," but on a sliding scale of values ranging from "not passable" to "outstanding." As a matter of fact, it is possible to achieve a relatively low score without a single "incorrect" answer because of evident weakness in the qualities being measured.

Occasionally, an examination may consist entirely of an oral test – either an individual or a group oral. In such cases, information is sought concerning the technical knowledges and abilities of the candidate, since there has been no written examination for this purpose. More commonly, however, an oral test is used to supplement a written examination.

Who conducts interviews?

The composition of oral boards varies among different jurisdictions. In nearly all, a representative of the personnel department serves as chairman. One of the members of the board may be a representative of the department in which the candidate would work. In some cases, "outside experts" are used, and, frequently, a businessman or some other representative of the general public is asked to serve. Labor and management or other special groups may be represented. The aim is to secure the services of experts in the appropriate field.

However the board is composed, it is a good idea (and not at all improper or unethical) to ascertain in advance of the interview who the members are and what groups they represent. When you are introduced to them, you will have some idea of their backgrounds and interests, and at least you will not stutter and stammer over their names.

What should be done before the interview?

While knowledge about the board members is useful and takes some of the surprise element out of the interview, there is other preparation which is more substantive. It *is* possible to prepare for an oral interview – in several ways:

1) Keep a copy of your application and review it carefully before the interview

This may be the only document before the oral board, and the starting point of the interview. Know what education and experience you have listed there, and the sequence and dates of all of it. Sometimes the board will ask you to review the highlights of your experience for them; you should not have to hem and haw doing it.

2) Study the class specification and the examination announcement

Usually, the oral board has one or both of these to guide them. The qualities, characteristics or knowledges required by the position sought are stated in these documents. They offer valuable clues as to the nature of the oral interview. For example, if the job involves supervisory responsibilities, the announcement will usually indicate that knowledge of modern supervisory methods and the qualifications of the candidate as a supervisor will be tested. If so, you can expect such questions, frequently in the form of a hypothetical situation which you are expected to solve. NEVER go into an oral without knowledge of the duties and responsibilities of the job you seek.

3) Think through each qualification required

Try to visualize the kind of questions you would ask if you were a board member. How well could you answer them? Try especially to appraise your own knowledge and background in each area, *measured against the job sought*, and identify any areas in which you are weak. Be critical and realistic – do not flatter yourself.

4) Do some general reading in areas in which you feel you may be weak

For example, if the job involves supervision and your past experience has NOT, some general reading in supervisory methods and practices, particularly in the field of human relations, might be useful. Do NOT study agency procedures or detailed manuals. The oral board will be testing your understanding and capacity, not your memory.

5) Get a good night's sleep and watch your general health and mental attitude

You will want a clear head at the interview. Take care of a cold or any other minor ailment, and of course, no hangovers.

What should be done on the day of the interview?

Now comes the day of the interview itself. Give yourself plenty of time to get there. Plan to arrive somewhat ahead of the scheduled time, particularly if your appointment is in the fore part of the day. If a previous candidate fails to appear, the board might be ready for you a bit early. By early afternoon an oral board is almost invariably behind schedule if there are many candidates, and you may have to wait.

Take along a book or magazine to read, or your application to review, but leave any extraneous material in the waiting room when you go in for your interview. In any event, relax and compose yourself.

The matter of dress is important. The board is forming impressions about you – from your experience, your manners, your attitude, and your appearance. Give your personal appearance careful attention. Dress your best, but not your flashiest. Choose conservative, appropriate clothing, and be sure it is immaculate. This is a business interview, and your appearance should indicate that you regard it as such. Besides, being well groomed and properly dressed will help boost your confidence.

Sooner or later, someone will call your name and escort you into the interview room. *This is it.* From here on you are on your own. It is too late for any more preparation. But remember, you asked for this opportunity to prove your fitness, and you are here because your request was granted.

What happens when you go in?

The usual sequence of events will be as follows: The clerk (who is often the board stenographer) will introduce you to the chairman of the oral board, who will introduce you to the other members of the board. Acknowledge the introductions before you sit down. Do not be surprised if you find a microphone facing you or a stenotypist sitting by. Oral interviews are usually recorded in the event of an appeal or other review.

Usually the chairman of the board will open the interview by reviewing the highlights of your education and work experience from your application – primarily for the benefit of the other members of the board, as well as to get the material into the record. Do not interrupt or comment unless there is an error or significant misinterpretation; if that is the case, do not hesitate. But do not quibble about insignificant matters. Also, he will usually ask you some question about your education, experience or your present job – partly to get you to start talking and to establish the interviewing "rapport." He may start the actual questioning, or turn it over to one of the other members. Frequently, each member undertakes the questioning on a particular area, one in which he is perhaps most competent, so you can expect each member to participate in the examination. Because time is limited, you may also expect some rather abrupt switches in the direction the questioning takes, so do not be upset by it. Normally, a board member will not pursue a single line of questioning unless he discovers a particular strength or weakness.

After each member has participated, the chairman will usually ask whether any member has any further questions, then will ask you if you have anything you wish to add. Unless you are expecting this question, it may floor you. Worse, it may start you off on an extended, extemporaneous speech. The board is not usually seeking more information. The question is principally to offer you a last opportunity to present further qualifications or to indicate that you have nothing to add. So, if you feel that a significant qualification or characteristic has been overlooked, it is proper to point it out in a sentence or so. Do not compliment the board on the thoroughness of their examination – they have been sketchy, and you know it. If you wish, merely say, "No thank you, I have nothing further to add." This is a point where you can "talk yourself out" of a good impression or fail to present an important bit of information. Remember, *you close the interview yourself.*

The chairman will then say, "That is all, Mr. _____, thank you." Do not be startled; the interview is over, and quicker than you think. Thank him, gather your belongings and take your leave. Save your sigh of relief for the other side of the door.

How to put your best foot forward

Throughout this entire process, you may feel that the board individually and collectively is trying to pierce your defenses, seek out your hidden weaknesses and embarrass and confuse you. Actually, this is not true. They are obliged to make an appraisal of your qualifications for the job you are seeking, and they want to see you in your best light. Remember, they must interview all candidates and a non-cooperative candidate may become a failure in spite of their best efforts to bring out his qualifications. Here are 15 suggestions that will help you:

1) Be natural – Keep your attitude confident, not cocky

If you are not confident that you can do the job, do not expect the board to be. Do not apologize for your weaknesses, try to bring out your strong points. The board is interested in a positive, not negative, presentation. Cockiness will antagonize any board member and make him wonder if you are covering up a weakness by a false show of strength.

2) Get comfortable, but don't lounge or sprawl

Sit erectly but not stiffly. A careless posture may lead the board to conclude that you are careless in other things, or at least that you are not impressed by the importance of the occasion. Either conclusion is natural, even if incorrect. Do not fuss with your clothing, a pencil or an ashtray. Your hands may occasionally be useful to emphasize a point; do not let them become a point of distraction.

3) Do not wisecrack or make small talk

This is a serious situation, and your attitude should show that you consider it as such. Further, the time of the board is limited – they do not want to waste it, and neither should you.

4) Do not exaggerate your experience or abilities

In the first place, from information in the application or other interviews and sources, the board may know more about you than you think. Secondly, you probably will not get away with it. An experienced board is rather adept at spotting such a situation, so do not take the chance.

5) If you know a board member, do not make a point of it, yet do not hide it

Certainly you are not fooling him, and probably not the other members of the board. Do not try to take advantage of your acquaintanceship – it will probably do you little good.

6) Do not dominate the interview

Let the board do that. They will give you the clues – do not assume that you have to do all the talking. Realize that the board has a number of questions to ask you, and do not try to take up all the interview time by showing off your extensive knowledge of the answer to the first one.

7) Be attentive

You only have 20 minutes or so, and you should keep your attention at its sharpest throughout. When a member is addressing a problem or question to you, give him your undivided attention. Address your reply principally to him, but do not exclude the other board members.

8) Do not interrupt

A board member may be stating a problem for you to analyze. He will ask you a question when the time comes. Let him state the problem, and wait for the question.

9) Make sure you understand the question

Do not try to answer until you are sure what the question is. If it is not clear, restate it in your own words or ask the board member to clarify it for you. However, do not haggle about minor elements.

10) Reply promptly but not hastily

A common entry on oral board rating sheets is "candidate responded readily," or "candidate hesitated in replies." Respond as promptly and quickly as you can, but do not jump to a hasty, ill-considered answer.

11) Do not be peremptory in your answers

A brief answer is proper – but do not fire your answer back. That is a losing game from your point of view. The board member can probably ask questions much faster than you can answer them.

12) Do not try to create the answer you think the board member wants

He is interested in what kind of mind you have and how it works – not in playing games. Furthermore, he can usually spot this practice and will actually grade you down on it.

13) Do not switch sides in your reply merely to agree with a board member

Frequently, a member will take a contrary position merely to draw you out and to see if you are willing and able to defend your point of view. Do not start a debate, yet do not surrender a good position. If a position is worth taking, it is worth defending.

14) Do not be afraid to admit an error in judgment if you are shown to be wrong

The board knows that you are forced to reply without any opportunity for careful consideration. Your answer may be demonstrably wrong. If so, admit it and get on with the interview.

15) Do not dwell at length on your present job

The opening question may relate to your present assignment. Answer the question but do not go into an extended discussion. You are being examined for a *new* job, not your present one. As a matter of fact, try to phrase ALL your answers in terms of the job for which you are being examined.

Basis of Rating

Probably you will forget most of these "do's" and "don'ts" when you walk into the oral interview room. Even remembering them all will not ensure you a passing grade. Perhaps you did not have the qualifications in the first place. But remembering them will help you to put your best foot forward, without treading on the toes of the board members.

Rumor and popular opinion to the contrary notwithstanding, an oral board wants you to make the best appearance possible. They know you are under pressure – but they also want to see how you respond to it as a guide to what your reaction would be under the pressures of the job you seek. They will be influenced by the degree of poise you display, the personal traits you show and the manner in which you respond.

EXAMINATION SECTION

EXAMINATION SECTION
TEST 1

DIRECTIONS: Each question or incomplete statement is followed by several suggested answers or completions. Select the one that BEST answers the question or completes the statement. *PRINT THE LETTER OF THE CORRECT ANSWER IN THE SPACE AT THE RIGHT.*

1. A book about the life of another person is called a(n)   1._____

    A. monograph   B. fiction   C. biography
    D. autobiography   E. reference

2. A book about real experiences is usually referred to as a(n)   2._____

    A. reference   B. monograph   C. fiction
    D. non-fiction   E. autobiography

3. The Dewey Decimal system is a   3._____

    A. list of books, magazines, and non-print materials
    B. system for checking out books
    C. method for organizing materials on the same subject matter together
    D. system for filing cards
    E. system for networking

4. A catalog card reading MOVIE see MOTION PICTURE means: 4._____

    A. All books on movies will be found under the subject heading MOTION PICTURE
    B. Additional books on movies will be found under the subject heading MOTION PIC-TURE
    C. Another library has the motion picture holdings
    D. Materials are expected on motion pictures
    E. All materials on movies are circulating

5. A bibliography is a(n)   5._____

    A. encyclopedia   B. networking
    C. means of circulating materials   D. list of materials
    E. reference tool

6. An annotation is a(n)   6._____

    A. review   B. explanatory note   C. precis
    D. format   E. critique

7. AMERICAN REFERENCE BOOKS ANNUAL provides a   7._____

    A. comprehensive reviewing service of reference books published in the United States
    B. monthly periodical furnishing reviews of popular reference tools
    C. publisher's guide to monthly reviewing sources
    D. professional journal published by the American Library Association
    E. bibliography of bibliographies

8. An index is a(n)

    A.   table of contents
    C.   series of footnotes
    E.   guide to locate material
    B.   encyclopedia
    D.   bibliography

8.___

9. The library catalog is a(n)

    A.   shelf list
    B.   index to the materials collection
    C.   bibliography
    D.   system for reserves
    E.   collection of book orders

9.___

10. A shelf list is a

    A.   record of materials in a library
    B.   reserve list
    C.   weeding list
    D.   list of reference materials
    E.   bibliography of reference sources

10.___

11. Technical services include

    A.   acquisitions, cataloging, and materials preparation
    B.   reference work and user services
    C.   reader's advisory services
    D.   circulation and reference services
    E.   networking

11.___

12. A collection of materials such as pamphlets, clippings, or illustrations kept in special containers is referred to as a

    A.   card catalog
    D.   container collection
    B.   card file
    E.   clipping file
    C.   vertical file

12.___

13. An electromagnetic recording made for playback on a television set is referred to as a(n)

    A.   audio tape
    D.   superdisk
    B.   cassette
    E.   fiche
    C.   video-recording

13.___

14. A word, name, object, group of words, or acronym describing a subject is usually referred to as a

    A.   cross reference
    C.   nom de plume
    E.   catalog card
    B.   subject heading
    D.   serial

14.___

15. A collection of materials with restricted circulation usually found in college and university libraries is called a(n) _____ collection.

    A.   reserved materials
    D.   open stack
    B.   patron
    E.   rotating reserve
    C.   student

15.___

16. An independent publication of forty-nine pages or less, bound in paper covers, is called a

    A.   serial
    D.   pamphlet
    B.   monograph
    E.   fiche
    C.   microcard

16.___

17. Library work directly concerned with assistance to readers in securing information and in using library resources is termed   17.____

    A. circulation services   B. technical services
    C. reader's advisory services   D. user services
    E. networking

18. A three-dimensional representation of a real object reproduced in the original size or to scale is called a(n)   18.____

    A. model   B. film   C. microform
    D. ultrafiche   E. videotape

19. The act of filling out required forms to become an eligible library borrower is called   19.____

    A. serialization   B. direction   C. registration
    D. reference work   E. signing

20. A direction in a catalog that guides the user to related names or subjects is termed a _____ reference.   20.____

    A. shelf   B. see-also   C. title
    D. see   E. subject

21. A record of a work in the catalog under the title is called a   21.____

    A. subject card   B. number entry   C. author card
    D. subject entry   E. title entry

22. The printed scheme of a classification system is referred to as a   22.____

    A. classification schedule   B. numbering schedule
    C. lettering schedule   D. cutter number
    E. copyright

23. The entry of a work in the catalog under the subject heading is called a   23.____

    A. subject card   B. subject heading   C. subject entry
    D. reference entry   E. subject guide

24. The department in a library responsible for officially listing prospective borrowers is the _____ department.   24.____

    A. reference   B. registration   C. welcoming
    D. circulation   E. technical

25. Library work that deals with patrons and the use of the library collection is called _____ services.   25.____

    A. technical   B. reader   C. circulation
    D. reference   E. public

KEY (CORRECT ANSWERS)

1.	C		11.	A
2.	D		12.	C
3.	C		13.	C
4.	A		14.	B
5.	D		15.	A
6.	B		16.	D
7.	A		17.	D
8.	E		18.	A
9.	B		19.	C
10.	A		20.	B

21.	E
22.	A
23.	C
24.	B
25.	D

TEST 2

DIRECTIONS: Each question or incomplete statement is followed by several suggested answers or completions. Select the one that BEST answers the question or completes the statement. *PRINT THE LETTER OF THE CORRECT ANSWER IN THE SPACE AT THE RIGHT.*

1. Material held for a borrower for a limited time is termed _____ material.   1._____

   A. reference   B. reserved   C. circulation
   D. special   E. held

2. A notice sent to a borrower to remind him to return heldover due material is a(n)   2._____

   A. warning   B. notice   C. overdue notice
   D. warning notice   E. call slip

3. Material returned to the library before the date due is   3._____

   A. Penalized   B. returned   C. accepted
   D. unneeded   E. subject to examination

4. Real objects, specimens, or artifacts are called   4._____

   A. toys   B. realia   C. games
   D. opaque material   E. models

5. A film with a series of pictures in sequence which creates the illusion of motion when pro-   5._____
   jected is classified as a

   A. photogram   B. motion picture   C. videotape
   D. cassette   E. slide

6. Laying books on the shelves in proper order is called   6._____

   A. placing   B. weeding   C. reading   D. shifting   E. shelving

7. A publication issued in successive parts usually to be continued indefinitely is referred to   7._____
   as a

   A. paper   B. monograph C. serial   D. pamphlet   E. edition

8. A record of the loan of material is called a   8._____

   A. call slip   B. reserve   C. contract   D. copy   E. charge

9. Information arranged in tabular, outline, or graphic form on a sheet of paper is called a   9._____

   A. classification   B. charge   C. chart
   D. catalog   E. cartoon

10. The method used to lend materials to borrowers and maintain the necessary records is   10._____
    the _____ system.

    A. classification   B. circulation control   C. reference
    D. borrowing   E. returnable

11. Any entry, other than a subject entry, that is made in a catalog in addition to the main entry is called a(n)

    A. added entry   B. call number   C. central reference
    D. reference entry   E. explanatory entry

11.___

12. The record of the number of items charged out of a library is termed

    A. record statistics   B. circulation statistics
    C. circulation control   D. record control
    E. itemizing

12.___

13. A number assigned to each book or item as it is received by the library is referred to as a(n) _____ number.

    A. call   B. accession   C. entry
    D. acquisition   E. ordering

13.___

14. A master file of all registered borrowers in a library system is called the _____ file.

    A. personnel   B. charging   C. classification
    D. central registration   E. circulation control

14.___

15. A person who charges out materials from a library is called the

    A. lender   B. technician   C. professional librarian
    D. clerk   E. borrower

15.___

16. A catalog in which all entries are filed in alphabetical order is called a(n) _____ catalog.

    A. card   B. Library of Congress   C. alphabetical
    D. dictionary   E. subject

16.___

17. The day material is to be returned to a library is usually referred to as the _____ day.

    A. library   B. date-due   C. return
    D. book   E. library-due

17.___

18. The act of annulling the library's record of a loan is called

    A. discharging   B. cancelling   C. stamping
    D. recording   E. unloaning

18.___

19. The penalty charge for material returned after the date due is called a(n)

    A. charge   B. fine   C. tax   D. levy   E. arrangement

19.___

20. A set of materials containing rules designed to be played in a competitive situation is called a

    A. rolodome   B. game   C. sketch   D. linedex   E. materialsset

20.___

21. A catalog in more than one part is termed a _____ catalog.

    A. divided   B. split   C. Library of Congress
    D. Dewey   E. Sears

21.___

22. A metal file containing a number of flat metal leaves that hold single cardboard strips list-   22.____
ing titles and holdings is called a

    A.   linedesk   B.   linetop   C.   rolotop
    D.   rotofile   E.   linedex

23. A metal file containing a number of shallow drawers in which serial check-in cards are   23.____
kept is usually referred to as a

    A.   linedesk   B.   rotofile   C.   box   D.   kardex   E.   linetop

24. The strip of paper pasted in the book or on the book packet, on which the date due is   24.____
stamped, is called the

    A.   date slip   B.   date card   C.   date strip
    D.   call slip   E.   card strip

25. Film on which materials have been photographed in greatly reduced size is called   25.____

    A.   minifilm   B.   microfilm   C.   photogram
    D.   miniaturization   E.   photoreduction

KEY (CORRECT ANSWERS)

1.	B		11.	A
2.	C		12.	B
3.	C		13.	B
4.	B		14.	D
5.	B		15.	E
6.	E		16.	D
7.	C		17.	B
8.	E		18.	A
9.	C		19.	B
10.	B		20.	B

21.	A
22.	E
23.	D
24.	A
25.	B

EXAMINATION SECTION

TEST 1

Questions 1-10.

DIRECTIONS: In Column II are some common library terms. In Column I are definitions for those terms. Match the terms to the definitions by placing the letter for the term in the space at the right of the corresponding definition.

COLUMN I

1. The slip upon which the request for a particular book is made

2. Reference made from one part of a book or card catalog to another where the same or allied subject is treated

3. Name given to a card in a catalog which lists the volumes of a series which library possesses

4. Refers to additional places to look

5. An entry for a part of a book

6. A list of books or articles on one particular subject

7. An entry for a series that has NOT ceased publication

8. Fiction

9. That part of a call number that refers to the author's name

10. Author's pen-name

COLUMN II

A. Analytical entry

B. Author number

C. Bibliography

D. Call slip

E. Cross reference

F. F

G. Library has

H. Open entry

I. Pseudonym

J. See also reference

1.____

2.____

3.____

4.____

5.____

6.____

7.____

8.____

9.____

10.____

Questions 11-20.

DIRECTIONS: Below you will find the titles or descriptions of
books with a list of possible words under which you
would find each in the card catalog. For each,
write the letter of the BEST answer in the space at
the right.

11.   The book entitled 100,000,000 GUINEA PIGS by Arthur   11.__
Kallet would be found in the drawer labeled
     A. Cam-Gof   B. Gag-Hal   C. Oat-Ote
     D. Laa-Mam   E. Peo-Pot

12.   A book entitled THE AMERICAN ROAD TO CULTURE will be   12.__
found in the drawer labeled
     A. Cou-Cut   B. The-Tho   C. Rho-Roe
     D. Ama-Ami   E. Ti-Tu

13.   A book entitled DR. PETE OF THE SIERRAS will be found in   13.__
the drawer labeled
     A. Doa-Doc   B. Pea-Pew   C. Dop-Dre
     D. Se-Sl   E. Oaf-Ote

14.   A book by Mazo De La Roche entitled THE BUILDING OF   14.__
JALNA:
     A. De La Roche   B. La Roche   C. Fiction
     D. Jalna   E. Carpentry

15.   A book by Antoine de Saint Exupery entitled WIND, SAND   15.__
AND STARS:
     A. de Saint Exupery   B. Antoine
     C. Saint Exupery   D. Exupery
     E. Sand

16.   A book by Wolfgang Ernst Langewiesche-Brandt entitled   16.__
STICK AND RUDDER and illustrated by Jo Kotula:
     A. Brandt   B. Langwiesche-Brandt
     C. Wolfgang   D. Ernst
     E. Kotula

17.   A book entitled FARTHER NORTH by Kathrene Sutherland   17.__
(Gedney) Pinkerton:
     A. North   B. Sutherland   C. Pinkerton
     D. Gedney   E. Kathrene

18.   A book entitled THE FORGE IN THE FOREST: 18.__
     A. Forge   B. Blacksmiths
     C. Forests and forestry   D. Forest
     E. Fiction

19.   A book by Raoul De Roussy de Sales entitled THE MAKING   19.__
OF TOMORROW:
     A. Tomorrow   B. Roussy de Sales
     C. De Roussy de Sales   D. de Sales
     E. Sales

20. A book by May Yonge McNeer entitled THE STORY OF THE
GREAT PLAINS:
    A. Yan-Yos   B. Mac-Mag   C. Nea-Neh
    D. Gor-Gui   E. Pit-Poe

20.___

Questions 21-25.

DIRECTIONS: Each of the following statements lists a topic on
which you might wish to find a book, together with
the possible word under which to look for it in the
card catalog. For each, write the letter of the BEST
answer in the space at the right.

21. Frontier and pioneer life
    A. Border life
    B. Frontier and pioneer life
    C. Pioneer life
    D. Adventure and adventurers
    E. Ranch life

21.___

22. Diesel engines
    A. Engines   B. Diesel engines
    C. Gas and oil engines   D. Motors
    E. Locomotives

22.___

23. Community centers
    A. Play centers   B. Recreation centers
    C. Social problems   D. Social settlements
    E. Community centers

23.___

24. Chemical industries
    A. Chemical technology   B. Industrial chemistry
    C. Technical chemistry   D. Chemistry, Technical
    E. Engineering chemistry

24.___

25. Cotton boll weevil
    A. Mexican boll weevil   B. Boll weevil
    C. Pests   D. Weevils
    E. Insects

25.___

KEY (CORRECT ANSWERS)

1. D		11. C	
2. E		12. D	
3. G		13. A	
4. J		14. A	
5. A		15. C	
6. C		16. B	
7. H		17. C	
8. F		18. A	
9. B		19. C	
10. I		20. B	

21. B
22. B
23. E
24. D

TEST 2

Questions 1-19.

DIRECTIONS: Each question consists of a statement. You are to indicate whether the statement is TRUE (T) or FALSE (F). *PRINT THE LETTER OF THE CORRECT ANSWER IN THE SPACE AT THE RIGHT.*

1. The CONGRESSIONAL DIRECTORY is a government document.   1.__

2. CURRENT BIOGRAPHY contains biographies of persons both living and dead.   2.__

3. The ENCYCLOPEDIA AMERICANA is more scholarly than the ENCYCLOPAEDIA BRITANNICA.   3.__

4. Unusual and obsolete words may be found below the line in the NEW STANDARD DICTIONARY.   4.__

5. The biography of the prime minister of England will be found in WHO'S WHO IN AMERICA.   5.__

6. If you look up Robert Louis Stevenson in the dictionary and in the encyclopedia, the LONGER account will be found in the dictionary.   6.__

7. The STATESMAN'S YEARBOOK contains no biographical notes.   7.__

8. The WORLD ALMANAC is a book of facts published annually.   8.__

9. LARNED'S NEW HISTORY FOR READY REFERENCE is a good source for recent world events.   9.__

10. To use WHO'S WHO IN AMERICA, one must consult the index.   10.__

11. The READERS' GUIDE contains digests of magazine articles.   11.__

12. Three important points to consider when buying an encyclopedia are: date, reliability, and arrangement.   12.__

13. The *fact index* is a feature of COMPTON'S PICTURED ENCYCLOPEDIA.   13.__

14. Biography is NOT a feature of the STATESMAN'S YEARBOOK.   14.__

15. The WORLD BOOK ENCYCLOPEDIA contains no illustrations.   15.__

16. The LINCOLN LIBRARY OF ESSENTIAL INFORMATION is arranged alphabetically.   16.__

17. The CONGRESSIONAL DIRECTORY contains biographies of government officials. 17.___

18. The index in BARTLETT'S FAMILIAR QUOTATIONS is by subject. 18.___

19. To use the WORLD ALMANAC, one must consult the index. 19.___

Questions 20-25.

DIRECTIONS: Each question or incomplete statement is followed by several suggested answers or completions. Select the one that BEST answers the question or completes the statement. *PRINT THE LETTER OF THE CORRECT ANSWER IN THE SPACE AT THE RIGHT.*

20. The word *Quisling* is found in WEBSTER'S NEW INTERNATIONAL 20.___
    DICTIONARY, 2nd ed. in
    A. the main alphabet
    B. Gazetteer
    C. new words section
    D. main alphabet below the line
    E. biographical dictionary

21. A biography of the composer Rossini may be found in 21.___
    A. WHO'S WHO IN AMERICA
    B. CURRENT BIOGRAPHY
    C. GRANGER'S INDEX TO POETRY AND RECITATIONS
    D. GROVE'S DICTIONARY OF MUSIC AND MUSICIANS
    E. READERS' GUIDE

22. For a map of Iran, one should consult 22.___
    A. WORLD ALMANAC
    B. STATESMAN'S YEARBOOK
    C. U.S. GOVERNMENT MANUAL
    D. RAND-McNALLY WORLD ATLAS
    E. WEBSTER'S NEW INTERNATIONAL DICTIONARY

23. A note on Jan Christian Smuts may be found in WEBSTER'S 23.___
    NEW INTERNATIONAL DICTIONARY in
    A. Gazetteer
    B. main alphabet
    C. pronouncing biographical dictionary
    D. new words
    E. abbreviations

24. For an article on radio showing diagrams of a receiver 24.___
    set, one should consult
    A. the librarian
    B. NEW INTERNATIONAL DICTIONARY
    C. STATESMAN'S YEARBOOK
    D. COMPTON'S PICTURED ENCYCLOPEDIA
    E. a newspaper

25. Statistics showing the cost and extent of irrigation in   25.___
    the United States may be found in
    A. STATESMAN'S YEARBOOK   B. WORLD ALMANAC
    C. CONGRESSIONAL DIRECTORY D. U.S. GOVERNMENT MANUAL
    E. CURRENT BIOGRAPHY

———

KEY (CORRECT ANSWERS)

1. T		11. F	
2. T		12. T	
3. F		13. T	
4. F		14. T	
5. F		15. F	
6. F		16. F	
7. F		17. T	
8. T		18. T	
9. F		19. T	
10. F		20. C	

21. D
22. D
23. C
24. D
25. B

———

TEST 3

Questions 1-10.

DIRECTIONS: The following entries appear in the READERS' GUIDE for June 1986 - October 1986. By means of them, you could find articles in magazines. Letters have been placed in parentheses above portions of the information contained in the entries. Below are questions about the entries. Answer them by writing the letters of the CORRECT item from the READERS' GUIDE in the space at the right. For each, use *one* letter *only* and do NOT use the same letter twice.

(A)
Close, Upton, pseud. See Hall, J.W.

(B)
Cochran, Phillip G.
                                    (C)
    Aerial invasion of Burma. H.H. Arnold. il pors Nat Geo
      Mag 86: 129-48 Ag '86
                          (D)
    Amazing adventures of Flip and Phil. por Am Mag 138: 121 Jl '86

(E)
Irving, Washington
                                    (F)
    World of Washington Irving. V. Brooks. Atlan 173: 134-86 Je;
      174: 135-86 J 174; 135-86 Jl; 138-86 Ag; 139-48 S; 139-48 O '86

(G)
Kid sister; story. See Schweitzer, G.

(H)
Packing industry
  Meat rate row; ICC proposal to cut freight rates on east-west
    meat hauls.
                  (I)   (J)
      meat hauls. Bsns W p24+Jl 22 '86

1. What person is the subject of an article?   1.____

2. Find the title of a story.   2.____

3. Find an author entry.   3.____

4. What symbol is used to indicate that the paging is NOT 4.____
    inclusive?

5. Find a subject entry.   5.____

6. Find an illustrated article.   6. __

7. Find an article that includes a portrait of the subject.   7. __

8. What pen-name is listed?   8. __

9. What is the title of a weekly magazine?   9. __

10. Find an article continued in succeeding issues of a   10. __
    magazine.

Questions 11-25.

DIRECTIONS: Each question consists of a statement. You are to
            indicate whether the statement is TRUE (T) or FALSE (F).
            *PRINT THE LETTER OF THE CORRECT ANSWER IN THE SPACE AT
            THE RIGHT.*

11. The appendix of a book contains additional material not   11. __
    included in the text of a book.

12. The full name of the publisher is found on the title page.   12. __

13. If one wishes to learn quickly on which page a certain   13. __
    item appears, he should consult the bibliography.

14. The date at the bottom of a title page always tells how   14. __
    old the material is in the book.

15. The author of a book is the person who has written it.   15. __

16. The preface lists in strict alphabetical order all the   16. __
    important topics, names, and terms which are discussed
    in a book.

17. No book should be carried from the library until it is   17. __
    signed for and stamped.

18. Fiction books frequently have indexes.   18. __

19. It is of no importance to know the name and publisher of   19. __
    a book.

20. The index of a book is usually in the back.   20. __

21. The QUICKEST way to find material in a reference book   21. __
    that is not indexed is to consult the introduction.

22. The index is an alphabetical list of the things described,   22. __
    explained, or alluded to in a book, with the numbers of
    the pages on which they are mentioned.

23. The introduction of a book gives a general discussion   23.___
of the subject matter of the book, preparing the reader
for the material taken up in the body of the book.

24. The copyright date and the date of publication are   24.___
always the same.

25. The number of the edition of a book usually appears on   25.___
the reverse of the title page.

———

KEY (CORRECT ANSWERS)

1. E	11. T
2. G	12. T
3. B	13. F
4. J	14. F
5. H	15. T
6. C	16. F
7. D	17. T
8. A	18. F
9. I	19. F
10. F	20. T

21. F
22. T
23. T
24. F
25. T

———

EXAMINATION SECTION
TEST 1

DIRECTIONS: Each question or incomplete statement is followed by several suggested answers or completions. Select the one that BEST answers the question or completes the statement. *PRINT THE LETTER OF THE CORRECT ANSWER IN THE SPACE AT THE RIGHT.*

Questions 1-5.

DIRECTIONS: Questions 1 through 5 are based on the entry below from the READERS' GUIDE TO PERIODICAL LITERATURE. For each question, select the word or expression that BEST completes the statement or answers the question.

Radioactive waste disposal
    A blow to nuclear power [Supreme Court ruling on atomic wastes]
    A. Press. il map NEWSWEEK 101:67-8 My 2 '83

    Needed: a garbage dump. H. Anderson. il NEWSWEEK 101:68 My 2 '83

    Nuclear industry takes it on the chin again [Supreme Court ruling that states may impose moratorium on nuclear power plant construction] il U.S. NEWS WORLD REP 94:8 My 2 '83

    Short circuit [Supreme Court upholds California ban on certification of nuclear facilities] il TIME 121:26 My 2 '83

Radioactive waste disposal in the ocean
    New radioactive waste law. OCEANS 16:70 Mr/Ap '83

1. In the entry *New radioactive waste law,* the number 70 designates the   1._____

    A. year the magazine was first published
    B. publisher's code number
    C. page number of the article
    D. volume number of the magazine

2. Which article has no accompanying photographs, maps or charts?   2._____

    A. *A blow to nuclear power*
    B. *Needed: a garbage dump*
    C. *Short circuit*
    D. *New radioactive waste law*

3. How are the articles under *Radioactive waste disposal* arranged?   3._____
    Alphabetically, by

    A. subject   B. title
    C. author's last name   D. magazine title

4. The entry *Short circuit* differs from the entry *Needed: a garbage dump* in that the entry   4._____
    Short circuit

    A. has a subtitle   B. gives no author's name
    C. was published earlier   D. appears on more pages

5. What is the function of the words within the brackets in the first entry? They

    A. give the title of the article
    B. indicate that the Supreme Court approved the article
    C. tell about the contents of the article
    D. show that the article is an editorial

5.__

Questions 6-10.

DIRECTIONS: In each group of sentences below the same idea is expressed in four different ways. For each group, select the way that is BEST.

    Privacy, Right of
      See also

      Confidential communications
      Wiretapping

      Count us out [West German census challenged on privacy grounds] TIME 121:37 Ap 25 '83

      NASA sets medical privacy rule [astronauts] C. Covault, AVIAT WEEK SPACE TECHNOL 118:14-15 Mr 28 '83

      Tales of a computer state. D. Burnham. NATION 236:527+ Ap 30 '83

      Wanted: right to privacy for children. G.B. Melton. il PSYCHOL TODAY 17:78-9 Mr '83

6. What is the title of the first article listed?

    A. Count us out
    B. Wiretapping
    C. Confidential communications
    D. West German census challenged on privacy grounds

6.__

7. Which article listed was published most recently?

    A. Count us out
    B. NASA sets medical privacy rule
    C. Tales of a computer state
    D. Wanted: right to privacy for children

7.__

8. The words enclosed in brackets are called

    A. footnotes   B. annotations
    C. synopses   D. definitions

8.__

9. On which page or pages would *Tales of a computer state* be found?　　9.____

    A. From page 236 to page 527
    B. On page 236 only
    C. On page 527 only
    D. On page 527 and following

10. Which is the only article with an illustration?　　10.____

    A. Count us out
    B. NASA sets medical privacy rule
    C. Tales of a computer state
    D. Wanted: right to privacy for children

Questions 11-15.

DIRECTIONS:　Questions 11 through 15 are based on the entry below from the READERS' GUIDE TO PERIODICAL LITERATURE. For each question, select the word or expression that BEST completes the statement or answers the question.

Federal Reserve System (U.S.)
    The Fed's next move on interest rates. M.W. Karmin.
      il U.S. NEWS WORLD REP 94:53 Ap 25 '83
    A fight with the Fed [defining a bank] il FORTUNE 107:72
      Mr 21 '83
    Is inflation coming back? A.F. Ehrbar, il FORTUNE 107:60-3
      Mr 21 '83
    More double talk at the Fed. M. Friedman. il NEWSWEEK
      101:72 My 2 '83
    The power of the Fed. M. Breibart and G. Epstein. il
      PROGRESSIVE 47:31-5 Ap '83
    The slow war on float. E. Spragins. il FORBES 131:116+
      Mr 28 '83
    Topic A in the money world [reappointment of P.A. Volcker].
      J.S. DeMott. il TIME 121:96-7 Ap 25 '83
    Washington Debate: Paul Volcker's report card. il BUSWEEK
      p114-15 My 2 '83

11. Which publication carried an article about Volcker?　　11.____

    A. TIME　　　　　　　　B. FORTUNE
    C. PROGRESSIVE　　　　D. NEWSWEEK

12. For which publication is no volume number given?　　12.____

    A. U.S. NEWS AND WORLD REPORT
    B. FORTUNE
    C. BUSINESS WEEK
    D. TIME

13. The number 60 in the listing for Ehrbar's article refers to the

    A. magazine's volume number
    B. number of pages in the magazine
    C. number of the page on which the article appears
    D. number of pages in the article

13._

14. Which publication has two articles listed from the same issue?

    A. NEWSWEEK   B. BUSINESS WEEK
    C. FORBES   D. FORTUNE

14._

15. Who is the author of the article that would be MOST likely to give information on the trends in interest rates?

    A. A.F. Ehrbar   B. M.W. Karmin
    C. E. Spragins   D. J.S. DeMott

15._

16. Arachne was the Greek goddess of weaving. Therefore, to which insect would the term *arachnid* MOST likely refer?

    A. Fly   B. Moth   C. Spider   D. Grasshopper

16._

17. The writer of a newspaper story is identified by the

    A. byline   B. headline   C. lead   D. caption

17._

18. Which name is closely linked to television ratings?

    A. Gallup   B. Nielsen   C. Nobel   D. Pulitzer

18._

19. Which word came into the English language from the Far East?

    A. Depot   B. Yacht   C. Kimono   D. Argosy

19._

20. One important purpose of a bibliography is to

    A. describe the author's background
    B. refer the reader to additional sources of information
    C. explain the special terms used in the book
    D. provide supplementary statistical material

20._

21. What is an anthology?
A

    A. collection of literary works
    B. list of synonyms and antonyms
    C. selection of famous quotations
    D. set of rules for punctuation

21._

Questions 22-30.

DIRECTIONS: In each group of sentences below, the same idea is expressed in four different ways. For each group, select the way that is BEST.

22. A. To be an excellent shortstop, a baseball player needs quick reflexes and a good throwing arm.

  B. Having a good throwing arm and needing quick reflexes, a baseball player can be an excellent shortstop.

  C. To be an excellent shortstop, a baseball player needs quick reflexes and have a good throwing arm.

  D. A baseball player needs quick reflexes to be an excellent shortstop and a good throwing arm.

22._____

23. A. He found his blanket on the chair, his shoes under the dresser, with a dusty floor.

  B. He found his blanket on the chair, his shoes under the dresser, and dust on the floor.

  C. He found his blanket on the chair, his shoes under the dresser, with the floor dusty.

  D. He found his blanket on the chair, his shoes under the dresser, and the floor needing dusting.

23._____

24. A. "I'm sure," she commented with a smile, "that you will all do a fine job."

  B. "I'm sure" she commented with a smile "that you will all do a fine job."

  C. I'm sure, "she commented with a smile," that you will all do a fine job.

  D. "I'm sure" she commented with a smile, "that you will all do a fine job."

24._____

25. A. These words are identical in pronunciation: they differ in spelling and meaning.

  B. These words are identical in pronunciation, they differ in spelling and meaning.

  C. These words are identical in pronunciation they differ in spelling and meaning.

  D. These words are identical in pronunciation; they differ in spelling and meaning.

25._____

26. A. All our friend's home's have central air-conditioning.

  B. All our friends' homes have central air-conditioning.

  C. All our friends home's have central air-conditioning.

  D. All our friends homes' have central air-conditioning.

26._____

27. A. A good writer in an uncommon way can express the commonplace.

  B. A good writer who can express it in an uncommon way expresses the common-place.

  C. A good writer can express in an uncommon way, the commonplace.

  D. A good writer is one who can express the commonplace in an uncommon way.

27._____

28. A. She has a strong faith both in youth and in education.

  B. She has a strong faith in both youth and in education.

  C. She has both a strong faith in youth and education.

  D. She has a strong faith in both youth and education.

28._____

29. A. The climax of the story occurs when the train leaves before the refugees can get to the station.

    B. The climax of the story is when the train leaves before the refugees can get to the station.

    C. The climax of the story occurs where the train leaves before the refugees can get to the station.

    D. The climax of the story is because the train leaves before the refugees can get to the station.

29.__

30. A. Having lost their way in the forest, Hansel and Gretal found lodging with the witch in the gingerbread house.

    B. Having lost their way in the forest, the witch in the gingerbread house gave Hansel and Gretel lodging.

    C. Having lost their way in the forest, the witch's gingerbread house gave Hansel and Gretel lodging.

    D. Having lost their way in the forest, lodging was given to Hansel and Gretel in the gingerbread house of the witch.

30.__

31. The copyright date of any book is found on the

    A. back of the cover
    B. index page
    C. reverse side of the title page
    D. last page of the bibliography

31.__

32. One characteristic common to television docudramas is that they

    A. are shown as a miniseries
    B. are about famous people
    C. dramatize historical novels
    D. contain elements of both truth and fiction

32.__

33. Which book is limited to facts about famous living Americans?

    A. WHO'S WHO IN AMERICA
    B. AMERICAN AUTHORS
    C. WORLD BOOK ENCYCLOPEDIA
    D. DICTIONARY OF AMERICAN BIOGRAPHY

33.__

34. Stage directions are suggestions about

    A. set design and construction
    B. tickets and properties
    C. expressions and movements
    D. rehearsals and performances

34.__

35. The connotation of a word refers to its

    A. literal meaning   B. common usage
    C. derivation   D. implied meaning

35.__

KEY (CORRECT ANSWERS)

1.	C		16.	C
2.	D		17.	A
3.	B		18.	B
4.	B		19.	C
5.	C		20.	B
6.	A		21.	A
7.	C		22.	A
8.	B		23.	B
9.	D		24.	A
10.	D		25.	D
11.	A		26.	B
12.	C		27.	D
13.	C		28.	D
14.	D		29.	A
15.	B		30.	A

31.	C
32.	D
33.	A
34.	C
35.	D

———

EXAMINATION SECTION
TEST 1

DIRECTIONS: Each question or incomplete statement is followed by several suggested answers or completions. Select the one that BEST answers the question or completes the statement. *PRINT THE LETTER OF THE CORRECT ANSWER IN THE SPACE AT THE RIGHT.*

1. An employee requests a book which is not in the department library.
   Of the following, the MOST advisable course of action for you to take is to

   A. attempt to get the book for him by means of the department's affiliation with the public library
   B. explain that the book is not available from the department's library
   C. suggest that he try his local public library and give him a list of local libraries
   D. tell him where he may purchase the book and offer to make the purchase for him

   1.____

2. The catalog for the use of department employees has just been thoroughly checked and revised by a professional librarian. After trying to find the name of a book in the catalog, an employee tells you that he cannot find it.
   Of the following, the MOST advisable action for you to take FIRST is to

   A. call the public library for the exact title
   B. look it up in the catalog yourself
   C. look through the stacks for the book
   D. tell him you are sorry but the book is not in the department library

   2.____

3. You find that three pages are missing from one of the copies of a very popular book in the department library.
   Of the following, the MOST advisable action for you to take is to

   A. discard the book since its usefulness is now sharply curtailed
   B. order another copy of the book but keep the old copy until the new one is received
   C. report the fact to the head of the department and request further instructions
   D. type copies of the pages from another volume of the book and tape them in the appropriate place

   3.____

4. The department library is scheduled to close at 5 P.M. It is now 4:55, and an employee reading a book shows no signs of leaving.
   Of the following, the MOST advisable action for you to take is to

   A. tell him it is time to leave
   B. tell him the time and ask him if he wishes to borrow the book
   C. turn the lights off and on, indirectly suggesting that he leave
   D. wait until he decides to leave

   4.____

5. The dealer from whom you have been buying books for the department library has informed you that henceforth he can give you only a fifteen percent instead of a twenty percent discount.
   Of the following, the MOST advisable course of action for you to take FIRST is to

   5.____

A.   accept the fifteen percent discount
B.   inform the head of your department
C.   investigate the discount given by other book dealers
D.   order directly from the publishers

6.   Your supervisor is a professional librarian and is responsible for the selection of material to be added to the department library in which you are an employee. Shortly after you start on the job, an employee of the department brings you a written request to have several books of his choice added to the library.
Of the following, the MOST advisable course of action for you to take is to

   6.___

A.   order the books immediately
B.   pass the suggestion along to your supervisor
C.   refuse to accept his suggestion
D.   tell him that he will have to buy the books

7.   You object to your supervisor's plan to change the system in the department library from closed to open stacks.
Of the following, the MOST advisable course of action for you to take is to

   7.___

A.   ask other members of the staff to support your objections
B.   await further instructions and then do as you are told
C.   discuss your objections with your supervisor
D.   send a brief report of your objections to the department head

8.   Two weeks after you begin working in the department library, you learn that books in library bindings last twice as long as those with the publishers' bindings.
Of the following, the MOST advisable course of action for you to follow is to

   8.___

A.   buy only paperbound books
B.   have all new books put in library bindings
C.   put in library bindings only rare editions
D.   put in library bindings only those books likely to get hard use

9.   Your superior is away on an official trip. You have been asked to type several hundred catalog cards before he returns. Just as you begin the job, the typewriter breaks down.
Of the following, the MOST advisable course of action for you to take is to

   9.___

A.   arrange to have the typewriter repaired as soon as possible
B.   do the cards by hand
C.   postpone the job until after your supervisor returns
D.   write to your supervisor for advice

10.   Your supervisor in the department library is out for the day. You receive a telephone call from another city department asking if they may borrow one of the books in your library.
Of the following, the MOST advisable action for you to take FIRST is to tell the department

   10.___

A.   that books are not permitted out of the department
B.   that you will check and call back the next day
C.   to send a representative to inquire the next day
D.   to write a letter to the department head

11. Two months have passed since the head of the department has borrowed one of the
books in the department library. Of the following, the MOST advisable action for you to
take is to

    A. ask the department head if he wishes to keep the book out longer
    B. leave a note for the department head telling him that the book should be returned
immediately
    C. wait another month and then write the book off as lost
    D. wait until you receive another request for the book

11.____

12. Your supervisor tells you that he would like to have all old book cards replaced, all torn
pages mended, and the books put in good condition in all other respects by the following
day. You know that this is an impossible task.
Of the following, the MOST advisable course of action for you to take is to

    A. attempt to finish as much of the job as possible
    B. explain the difficulties involved to the supervisor and await further instruction
    C. ignore the request since it is completely unreasonable
    D. make a complaint to the head of the department

12.____

13. The library in which you work has received about fifty new books. These books must be
cataloged, but you have had no experience in this type of work. However, you have been
told that a professional librarian will join the staff in about six weeks.
Of the following, the MOST advisable course of action for you to take in the meantime
is to

    A. close the library for a week and try to do the cataloging yourself
    B. lend the books only to those who can get special permission
    C. let the users take the books even though they are not cataloged
    D. put all the books in storage until they can be cataloged

13.____

14. The hospital library in which you work has a large back-log of books that need to be
mended. You are unable to do more than a small part of the job by yourself. One of the
patients in the hospital has done book binding and mending. He offers to help you
because he sees the need for doing the job and because he wants something to do with
his hands.
Of the following, the MOST advisable course of action for you to take is to

    A. accept his offer on condition that the doctor approves
    B. ask him to push the book cart around the wards so you will be free to do the mend-
ing
    C. refuse his offer
    D. write a letter to his former employer to find out whether he is a good bookbinder

14.____

15. You accidentally spill a glass of water over an open book.
Of the following, the MOST advisable action for you to take FIRST in most cases is to

    A. discard the book to prevent the water from spoiling other material
    B. hang the book up by its binding
    C. press the covers together to squeeze out the water
    D. separate the wet pages with blotters

15.____

16. In mending a book, you overturn a jar of glue on a new book.   16.__
    Of the following, the MOST advisable action for you to take FIRST is to

    A. allow the glue to harden so that it may be peeled off
    B. attempt to wipe off the glue with any clean scrap paper
    C. discard the book to prevent other materials from being spoiled
    D. report the incident immediately to your supervisor

17. Of the following, the situation LEAST likely to result in injury to books is one in which   17.__

    A. all books support each other standing upright
    B. short books are placed between tall ones
    C. the books are as close together as possible
    D. the books lean against the sides of the shelves

18. Of the following, a damp cloth may BEST be used to clean a cloth book cover that has   18.__
    been coated with

    A. benzene   B. gold leaf
    C. turpentine   D. varnish

19. Decay of leather bindings may be MOST effectively delayed by   19.__

    A. a short tanning period
    B. air conditioning
    C. rubbing periodically with a damp cloth
    D. treatment with heat

20. When paste is used to mend a page, it is MOST desirable that the page should then be   20.__

    A. aired   B. heated   C. pressed   D. sprayed

21. A book that is perfectly clean but has been used by someone with chicken pox can prob-   21.__
    ably BEST be handled by

    A. burning, followed by proper disposal of the ashes
    B. forty-eight hour exposure to ultraviolet light
    C. keeping it out of circulation for six months
    D. treating it the same as any other book

22. The BEST combination of temperature and humidity for books is temperature _____   22.__
    degrees, humidity _____.

    A. 50-60; 20-30%   B. 60-70; 10-20%
    C. 60-70; 50-60%   D. 70-80; 70-80%

23. When a new book is received, it is LEAST important to keep a record of the   23.__

    A. author's name
    B. cost of the book
    C. number of pages
    D. source from which it was obtained

24. You have just received from the publisher a new book for the department library, but you find that the binding is torn.
Of the following, the MOST advisable action for you to take is to

    24.____

    A. mend the binding and take no further action
    B. mend the binding but claim a price discount
    C. report the damage to the department head
    D. send the book back to the publisher

25. Of the following, a characteristic of MOST photographic charging systems is that

    25.____

    A. book cards are not used
    B. charging is done by one person
    C. date due is stamped on borrower's card
    D. transaction cards are not used

_____

KEY (CORRECT ANSWERS)

1.	A		11.	A
2.	B		12.	B
3.	D		13.	C
4.	B		14.	A
5.	C		15.	D
6.	B		16.	B
7.	C		17.	A
8.	D		18.	D
9.	A		19.	B
10.	B		20.	C

21.	D
22.	C
23.	C
24.	D
25.	B

_____

TEST 2

DIRECTIONS: Each question or incomplete statement is followed by several suggested answers or completions. Select the one that BEST answers the question or completes the statement. *PRINT THE LETTER OF THE CORRECT ANSWER IN THE SPACE AT THE RIGHT.*

1. In a card catalog, a reference from one subject heading to another is MOST commonly called a(n) _____ reference.

    A. cross   B. direct   C. primary   D. indirect

1.___

2. A book which is shortened by omission of detail but which retains the general sense of the original is called a(n)

    A. compendium   B. manuscript
    C. miniature   D. abridgment

2.___

3. An anonymous book is a

    A. book published before 1500
    B. book whose author is unknown
    C. copy which is defective
    D. work that is out of print

3.___

4. All the letters, figures, and symbols assigned to a book to indicate its location on library shelves comprise the _____ number.

    A. call   B. Cutter   C. index   D. inventory

4.___

5. The term *format* does NOT refer to a book's

    A. binding   B. size
    C. theme   D. typography

5.___

6. The term *card catalog* USUALLY refers to a

    A. catalog consisting of loose-leaf pages upon which the cards are pasted
    B. catalog in which entries are on separate cards arranged in a definite order
    C. catalog of the cards available from the Library of Congress
    D. record on cards of the works which have been weeded out of the library collection

6.___

7. The term *circulation record* USUALLY refers to a record of

    A. daily attendance
    B. the books borrowed
    C. the most popular books
    D. the books out on interlibrary loan

7.___

8. Reading shelves USUALLY involves checking the shelves to see that all the books

    A. are in the correct order
    B. are suitable for the library's patrons
    C. are there
    D. have been cataloged correctly

8.___

9. In an alphabetical catalog of book titles and authors' names, the name *de Santis* would be filed   9._____

    A. after *DeWitt*
    B. after *Sanders*
    C. before AND THEN THERE WERE NONE
    D. before *Deutsch*

10. In typing catalog cards, the shift key on the typewriter would be used to   10._____

    A. change from black ribbon to red ribbon
    B. move the carriage from left to right
    C. move the carriage from right to left
    D. type capitals

11. The abbreviation e.g. means *most nearly*   11._____

    A. as follows
    C. refer to
    B. for example
    D. that is

12. The abbreviation ff. means *most nearly*   12._____

    A. and following pages
    C. frontispiece
    B. formerly
    D. the end

13. The abbreviation ibid, means *most nearly*   13._____

    A. consult the index
    C. see below
    B. in the same place
    D. turn the page

14. *Ex libris* is a Latin phrase meaning   14._____

    A. former librarian
    C. without charge
    B. from the books
    D. without liberty

15. An expurgated edition of a book is one which   15._____

    A. contains many printing errors
    B. includes undesirable passages
    C. is not permitted in public libraries
    D. omits objectionable material

16. The re-charging of a book to a borrower is USUALLY called   16._____

    A. fining
    C. reissue
    B. processing
    D. renewal

17. A sheet of paper that is pierced with holes is   17._____

    A. borated
    C. perforated
    B. collated
    D. serrated

18. *Glossary* means *most nearly* a(n)   18._____

    A. dictionary of selected terms in a particular book or field
    B. list of chapter headings in the order in which they appear in a book
    C. section of the repairing division which coats books with a protective lacquer
    D. alphabetical table of the contents of a book

19. *Accessioning* means *most nearly*

    A. acquiring books
    B. arranging books for easy access
    C. donating books as gifts
    D. listing books in the order of purchase

19.___

20. *Bookplate* means *most nearly*

    A. a label in a book showing who owns it
    B. a metal device for holding books upright
    C. a rounded zinc surface upon which a page is printed
    D. the flat part of the binding of a book

20.___

21. *Thesaurus* means *most nearly* a book which

    A. contains instructions on how to prepare a thesis
    B. contains words grouped according to similarity of meaning
    C. describes the techniques of dramatic acting
    D. gives quotations from well-known works of literature

21.___

22. *Salacious* means *most nearly*

    A. careful   B. delicious   C. lewd   D. salty

22.___

23. *Pseudonym* means *most nearly*

    A. false report   B. fictitious name
    C. libelous statement   D. psychic phenomenon

23.___

24. *Gamut* means *most nearly* a(n)

    A. bookworm   B. simpleton
    C. vagrant   D. entire range

24.___

25. *Monograph* means *most nearly* a

    A. machine for duplicating typewritten material by means of a stencil
    B. picture reproduced on an entire page of a manuscript
    C. single chart used to represent statistical data
    D. systematic treatise on a particular subject

25.___

KEY (CORRECT ANSWERS)

1.	A		11.	B
2.	D		12.	A
3.	B		13.	B
4.	A		14.	B
5.	C		15.	D
6.	B		16.	D
7.	B		17.	C
8.	A		18.	A
9.	D		19.	D
10.	D		20.	A

21.	B
22.	C
23.	B
24.	D
25.	D

———

TEST 3

DIRECTIONS: Each question or incomplete statement is followed by several suggested answers or completions. Select the one that BEST answers the question or completes the statement. *PRINT THE LETTER OF THE CORRECT ANSWER IN THE SPACE AT THE RIGHT.*

Questions 1-15.

DIRECTIONS: Questions 1 through 15 are to be answered SOLELY on the basis of the information contained in the following passage.

Machines may be useful for bibliographic purposes, but they will be useful only if we study the bibliographic requirements to be met and the machines available, in terms of each Job which needs to be done. Many standard tools now available are more efficient than high-speed machines if the machines are used as gadgets rather than as the mechanical elements of well-considered systems.

It does not appear impossible for us to learn to think in terms of scientific management to such an extent that we may eventually be able to do much of the routine part of bibliographic work mechanically with greater efficiency, both in terms of cost per unit of service and in terms of management of the intellectual content of literature. There are many bibliographic tasks which will probably not be done mechanically in the near future because the present tools appear to present great advantages over any machine in sight; for example, author bibliography done on the electronic machines would appear to require almost as much work in instructing the machine as is required to look in an author catalog. The major field of usefulness of the machines would appear to be that of subject bibliography, and particularly in research rather than quick reference jobs.

Machines now available or in sight cannot answer a quick reference question either as fast or as economically as will consultation of standard reference works such as dictionaries, encyclopedias, or almanacs, nor would it appear worthwhile to instruct a machine and run the machine to pick out one recent book or "any recent book" in a broad subject field. It would appear, therefore, that high-speed electronic or electrical machinery may be used for bibliographic purposes only in research institutions, at least for the next five or ten years, and their use will probably be limited to research problems in those institutions. It seems quite probable that during the next decade electronic machines, including the Rapid Selector, which was designed with bibliographic purposes in mind, will find application in administrative, office, and business uses to a much greater extent than they will in bibliographic operations.

The shortcomings of machines used as gadgets have been stressed in this paper. Nevertheless, the use of machines for bibliographic purposes is developing, and it is developing rapidly. It appears quite certain that several of the machines and mechanical devices can now perform certain of the routine operations involved in bibliographic work more accurately and more efficiently than these operations can be performed without them.

At least one machine, the Rapid Selector, appears potentially capable of performing higher orders of bibliographic work than we have been able to perform in the past, if and when we learn: (a) what is really needed for the advancement of learning in the way of bibliographic services; and (b) how to utilize the machine efficiently.

There is no magic in machines as such. There will be time-lag in their application, just as there was with the typewriter. The speed and efficiency in handling the mechanical part of bibliographic work, which will determine the point of diminishing returns, depend in large measure on how long it will be before we approach these problems from the point of view of scientific management.

This report cannot solve the problem of bibliographic organization. Machines alone cannot solve the problem. We need to develop systems of handling the mass of bibliographic material, but such systems cannot be developed until we discover and establish our objectives, our plans, our standards, our methods and controls, within the framework of each situation. This may take twenty years or it may take one hundred, but it will come. The termination of how long the time-lag will be rests upon our time-lag in gathering objective information upon which scientific management of literature can be based.

1. On the basis of the above passage, machines will *probably* be MOST useful in

   A. determining the cost per unit of service
   B. quick reference jobs
   C. subject bibliography
   D. title cataloging

1.____

2. On the basis of the above passage, the Rapid Selector will *probably* be LEAST used during the next ten years in

   A. administration   B. bibliographic work
   C. business   D. office work

2.____

3. It may be inferred from the above passage that is is NOT practical to use machines to do author bibliography because

   A. experienced machine operators are not available
   B. more than one machine is needed for such a task
   C. the results obtained from a machine are unreliable
   D. too much work is involved in instructing the machine

3.____

4. On the basis of the above passage, one of the criteria of efficiency is the

   A. amount of work required   B. cost per unit of service
   C. net cost of service   D. number of machines available

4.____

5. On the basis of the above passage, the LEAST efficient of the following for quick reference jobs are

   A. bibliographies   B. dictionaries
   C. encyclopedias   D. machines

5.____

6. On the basis of the above passage, in the next few years, high-speed electronic machinery will probably be used for bibliographic purposes only by

   A. civil engineers
   B. institutions of higher education
   C. publishers
   D. research institutions

6.____

7. On the basis of the above passage, the Rapid Selector was designed for use in handling   7.__

    A. bibliographic operations
    B. computing problems
    C. photographic reproduction
    D. standard reference works

8. On the basis of the above passage, progress on the development of machines to do bib-   8.__
liographic tasks has reached the point at which

    A. all present tools have become obsolete
    B. certain jobs are better performed with machines than without them
    C. machines are as efficient in doing quick reference jobs as in doing special research jobs
    D. machines are no longer regarded as being too expensive

9. The one of the following which is NOT stated by the above passage to be essential in   9.__
developing ways of handling bibliographic material is

    A. discovering methods and controls
    B. establishing objectives
    C. establishing standards
    D. obtaining historical data

10. The above passage indicates that machines alone will NOT be able to solve the problem   10.__
of

    A. bibliographic organization
    B. reference work
    C. scientific management
    D. system analysis

11. On the basis of the above passage, the viewpoint of scientific management is essential in   11.__

    A. developing the mechanical handling of bibliographic work
    B. operating the Rapid Selector
    C. repairing electronic machines
    D. showing that people are always superior to machines in bibliographic work

12. On the basis of the above passage, there are machines in existence which   12.__

    A. are particularly useful for statistical analysis in library work
    B. are the result of scientific management of bibliographic work
    C. have not been efficiently utilized for bibliographic work
    D. may be installed in a medium-sized library

13. On the basis of the above passage, the scientific management of literature awaits the   13.__

    A. assembling of objective information
    B. compilation of new reference books
    C. development of more complex machines
    D. development of simplified machinery

14. Based on the above passage, it may be INFERRED that the author's attitude toward the use of machines in bibliographic work is that they 14.____

    A.   have limited usefulness at the present time
    B.   will become useful only if scientific management is applied
    C.   will probably always be restricted to routine operations
    D.   will probably never be useful

15. The author of the above passage believes that high-speed machines are BEST adapted to bibliographic work when they are used 15.____

    A.   as gadgets
    B.   in place of standard reference works
    C.   to perform complex operations
    D.   to perform routine operations

Questions 16-25.

DIRECTIONS: Questions 16 through 25 deal with the classification of non-fiction books according to the Dewey Classification as outlined below. For each book listed, print in the space on the right the letter in front of the class to which it belongs.

<u>Classification</u>

16.	Ernst. WORDS: ENGLISH ROOTS AND HOW THEY GROW	A.	000 General Works	16.____
17.	Faulkner. FROM VERSAILLES TO THE NEW DEAL	B.	100 Philosophy	17.____
18.	Fry. CHINESE ART	C.	200 Religion	18.____
19.	Kant. CRITIQUE OF PURE REASON	D.	300 Social Science	19.____
20.	Millikan. THE ELECTRON	E.	400 Philology	20.____
21.	Morgan. THEORY OF THE GENE	F.	500 Pure Science	21.____
22.	Raine. THE YEAR ONE; POEMS	G.	600 Applied Science, Useful Arts	22.____
23.	Richards. PRINCIPLES OF LITERARY CRITICISM	H.	700 Fine Arts	23.____
24.	Steinberg. BASIC JUDAISM	I.	800 Literature, Belleslettres	24.____
25.	Strachey. QUEEN VICTORIA	J.	900 History, Biography	25.____

KEY (CORRECT ANSWERS)

1.	C	11.	A
2.	B	12.	C
3.	D	13.	A
4.	B	14.	A
5.	D	15.	D
6.	D	16.	E
7.	A	17.	J
8.	B	18.	H
9.	D	19.	B
10.	A	20.	F

21.	F
22.	I
23.	I
24.	C
25.	J

——————

READING COMPREHENSION
UNDERSTANDING AND INTERPRETING WRITTEN MATERIAL

EXAMINATION SECTION

DIRECTIONS: Each question or incomplete statement is followed by several suggested answers or completions. Select the one that BEST answers the question or completes the statement. *PRINT THE LETTER OF THE CORRECT ANSWER IN THE SPACE AT THE RIGHT.*

TEST 1

1. The question *Who shall now teach Hegel?* is shorthand for the question *Who is going to teach this genre - all the so-called Continental philosophers?* The obvious answer to this question is *Whoever cares to study them.* This is also the right answer, but we can only accept it whole-heartedly if we clear away a set of factitious questions. One such question is *Are these Continental philosophers really philosophers?* Analytic philosophers, because they identify philosophical ability with argumentative skill and notice that there is nothing they would consider an argument in the bulk of Heidegger or Foucault, suggest that these must be people who tried to be philosophers and failed--incompetent philosophers. This is as silly as saying that Plato was an incompetent sophist, or that a hedgehog is an incompetent fox. Hegel knew what he thought about philosophers who imitated the method and style of mathematics. He thought they were incompetent. These reciprocal charges of incompetence do nobody any good. We should just drop the questions of what philosophy really is or who really counts as a philosopher.
Which sentence is BEST supported by the above paragraph?
   A. The study of Hegel's philosophy is less popular now than in the past.
   B. Philosophers must stop questioning the competence of other philosophers.
   C. Philosophers should try to be as tolerant as Foucault and Heidegger.
   D. Analytic philosophers tend to be more argumentative than other philosophers.

1.____

2. It is an interesting question: the ease with which organizations of different kinds at different stages in their history can continue to function with ineffectual leadership at the top, or even function without a clear system of authority. Certainly, the success of some experiments in worker self-management shows that *bosses* are not always necessary, as some contemporary Marxists argue. Indeed, sometimes the function of those at the top is merely to symbolize organizational accountability, especially in dealing with outside authorities, but not to guide the actions of those within the organization. A vice president of a large insurance company remarked to us that *Presidents are powerless; no one needs them. They should all be sent*

2.____

off to do public relations for the company. While this is clearly a self-serving statement from someone next in line to command, it does give meaning to the expression *being kicked upstairs.*
According to the author,
A. organizations function very smoothly without bosses
B. the function of those at the top is sometimes only to symbolize organizational accountability
C. company presidents are often inept at guiding the actions of those within the organization
D. presidents of companies have less power than one might assume they have

3. The goal of a problem is a terminal expression one wishes to cause to exist in the world of the problem. There are two types of goals: specified goal expressions in proof problems and incompletely specified goal expressions in find problems. For example, consider the problem of finding the value of X, given the expression 4X + 5 = 17. In this problem, one can regard the goal expression as being of the form X = ___, the goal expression. The goal expression in a find problem of this type is incompletely specified. If the goal expression were specified completely – for example, X = 3 – then the problem would be a proof problem, with only the sequence of operations to be determined in order to solve the problem. Of course, if one were not guaranteed that the goal expression X = 3 was true, then the terminal goal expression should really be considered to be incompletely specified – something like the statement *X = 3 is (true or false).*
According to the preceding paragraph,
A. the goal of the equation 4X + 5 = 17 is true, not false
B. if the goal expression was specified as being equal to 3, the problem 4X + 5 = 17 would be a proof problem
C. if the sequence of operations of the problem given in the paragraph is predetermined, the goal of the problem becomes one of terminal expression, or the number 17
D. X cannot be found unless X is converted into a proof problem

4. We have human psychology and animal psychology, but no plant psychology. Why? Because we believe that plants have no perceptions or intentions. Some plants exhibit *behavior* and have been credited with *habits*. If you stroke the midrib of the compound leaf of a sensitive plant, the leaflets close. The sunflower changes with the diurnal changes in the source of light. The lowest animals have not much more complicated forms of behavior. The sea anemone traps and digests the small creatures that the water brings to it; the pitcher plant does the same thing and even more, for it presents a cup of liquid that attracts insects, instead of letting the surrounding medium drift them into its trap. Here as everywhere in nature where the great, general classes of living things diverge, the lines between them are not perfectly clear. A sponge is an animal; the pitcher plant is a flowering plant, but it comes nearer to

3. ___

4. ___

feeding itself than the animal. Yet the fact is that we credit all animals, and only the animals, with some degree of feeling.

Of the following, the MAIN idea expressed in the above paragraph is:
   A. The classification of plants has been based on beliefs about their capacity to perceive and feel
   B. Many plants are more evolved than species considered animals
   C. The lines that divide the classes of living things are never clear
   D. The abilities and qualities of plants are undervalued

5. Quantitative indexes are not necessarily adequate measures   5.___
   of true economic significance or influence. But even the
   raw quantitative data speak loudly of the importance of the
   new transnationalized economy. The United Nations estimates
   value added in this new sector of the world economy at $500
   billion in 1971, amounting to one-fifth of total GNP of the
   non-socialist world and exceeding the GNP of any one other
   country except the United States. Furthermore, all observers
   agree that the share of this sector in the world economy is
   growing rapidly. At least since 1950, its annual rate of
   growth has been high and remarkably steady at 10 percent
   compared to 4 percent for noninternationalized output in the
   Western developed countries. One spokesman for the new
   system frankly envisages that within a generation some
   400 to 500 multinational corporations will own close to two-
   thirds of the world's fixed assets.
   According to the author, all of the following are true
   EXCEPT:
      A. Quantitative indexes are not necessarily adequate measures of actual economic influence
      B. The transnational sector of the world economy is growing rapidly
      C. Since 1950, the rate of growth of transnationals has been 10% compared to 4% for internationalized output in the Western developed countries
      D. Continued growth for multinational corporations is likely

6. A bill may be sent to the Governor when it has passed   6.___
   both houses. During the session, he is given ten days
   to act on bills that reach his desk. Bills sent to him
   within ten days of the end of the session must be acted
   on within 30 days after the last day of the session. If
   the Governor takes no action on a ten day bill, it auto-
   matically becomes a law. If he disapproves or vetoes a
   ten day bill, it can become law only if it is re-passed
   by two-thirds vote in each house. If he fails to act on
   a 30 day bill, the bill is said to have received a *pocket
   veto*. It is customary for the Governor to act, however,
   on all bills submitted to him, and give his reason in
   writing for approving or disapproving important legislation.

According to the above paragraph, all of the following are
true EXCEPT:
   A. Bills sent to the Governor in the last ten days of the
      session must be acted on within thirty days after the
      last day of the session
   B. If the Governor takes no action on a 10 day bill, it
      is said to have received a *pocket veto*
   C. It is customary for the Governor to act on all bills
      submitted to him
   D. If the Governor vetoes a ten day bill, it can become
      law only if passed by a two-thirds vote of the
      Legislature

7. It is particularly when I see a child going through the   7.___
   mechanical process of manipulating numbers without any
   intuitive sense of what it is all about that I recall the
   lines of Lewis Carroll: *Reeling and Writhing, of course,*
   to begin with...and then the different branches of Arithmetic-
   Ambition, Distraction, Uglification, and Derision. Or, as
   Max Beberman has put it, much more gently: *Somewhat related*
   to the notion of discovery in teaching is our insistence that
   the student become aware of a concept before a name has been
   assigned to the concept. I am quite aware that the issue
   of intuitive understanding is a very live one among teachers
   of mathematics, and even a casual reading of the YEARBOOK of
   the National Council of Teachers of Mathematics makes it
   clear that they are also very mindful of the gap that exists
   between proclaiming the importance of such understanding
   and actually producing it in the classroom.
   The MAIN idea expressed in the above paragraph is:
   A. Math teachers are concerned about the difficulties
      inherent in producing an understanding of mathematics
      in their students
   B. It is important that an intuitive sense in approaching
      math problems be developed, rather than relying on
      rote, mechanical learning
   C. Mathematics, by its very nature, encourages rote,
      mechanical learning
   D. Lewis Carroll was absolutely correct in his assessment
      of the true nature of mathematics

8. Heisenberg's Principle of Uncertainty, which states that   8.___
   events at the atomic level cannot be observed with certain-
   ty, can be compared to this: in the world of everyday
   experience, we can observe any phenomenon and measure its
   properties without influencing the phenomenon in question
   to any significant extent. To be sure, if we try to
   measure the temperature of a demitasse with a bathtub
   thermometer, the instrument will absorb so much heat from
   the coffee that it will change the coffee's temperature
   substantially. But with a small chemical thermometer, we
   may get a sufficiently accurate reading. We can measure
   the temperature of a living cell with a miniature thermometer, which has almost negligible heat capacity.
   But in the atomic world, we can never overlook the dis-
   turbance caused by the introduction of the measuring
   apparatus.

Which sentence is BEST supported by the above paragraph?
   A. There is little we do not alter by the mere act of observation.
   B. It is always a good idea to use the smallest measuring device possible.
   C. Chemical thermometers are more accurate than bathtub thermometers.
   D. It is not possible to observe events at the atomic level and be sure that the same events would occur if we were not observing them.

9. It is a myth that American workers are pricing themselves   9.___
   out of the market, relative to workers in other industri-
   alized countries of the world. The wages of American
   manufacturing workers increased at a slower rate in the
   1970's than those of workers in other major western countries.
   In terms of American dollars, between 1970 and 1980, hourly
   compensation increased 489 percent in Japan and 464 percent
   in Germany, compared to 128 percent in the United States.
   Even though these countries experienced faster productivity
   growth, their unit labor costs still rose faster than in
   the United States, according to the Bureau of Labor Statistics. During the 1970's, unit labor costs rose 192 percent
   in Japan, 252 percent in Germany, and only 78 percent in
   the United States.
   According to the above passage,
   A. unit labor costs in the 1970's were higher in Japan
      than they were in Germany or the United States
   B. the wages of American workers need to be increased to
      be consistent with other countries
   C. American workers are more productive than Japanese or
      German workers
   D. the wages of American workers in manufacturing
      increased at a slower rate in the 1970's than the
      wages of workers in Japan or Germany

10. No people have invented more ways to enjoy life than the   10.___
    Chinese, perhaps to balance floods, famines, warlords, and
    other ills of fate. The clang of gongs, clashing cymbals,
    and beating of drums sound through their long history.
    No month is without fairs and theatricals when streets are
    hung with fantasies of painted lanterns and crowded with
    carriages that flow like water, horses like roaming dragons.
    Night skies are illumined by firecrackers - a Chinese
    invention - bursting in the form of flowerpots, peonies,
    fiery devils. The ways of pleasure are myriad. Music
    plays in the air through bamboo whistles of different pitch
    tied to the wings of circling pigeons. To skim a frozen
    lake in an ice sleigh with a group of friends on a day when
    the sun is warm is rapture, like *moving in a cup of jade.*
    What more delightful than the ancient festival called *Half
    an Immortal*, when everyone from palace officials to the
    common man took a ride on a swing? When high in the air,
    one felt like an Immortal, when back to earth once again
    human - no more than to be for an instant a god.

According to the above passage,
 A. if the Chinese hadn't had so many misfortunes, they wouldn't have created so many pleasurable pasttimes
 B. the Chinese invented flowerpots
 C. every month the Chinese have fairs and theatricals
 D. pigeons are required to play the game *Half an Immortal*

11. In our century, instead, poor Diphilus is lost in the   11. ___
crowd of his peers. We flood one another. No one recog-
nizes him as he loads his basket in the supermarket. What
grevious fits of melancholy have I not suffered in one of
our larger urban bookstores, gazing at the hundreds,
thousands, tens of thousands of books on shelves and tables?
And what are they to the hundreds of thousands, the millions
that stand in our research libraries? More books than Noah
saw raindrops. How many readers will read a given one of
them - mine, yours - in their lifetimes? And how will it
be in the distant future? Incomprehensible masses of books,
Pelion upon Ossa, hordes of books, each piteously calling
for attention, respect, love, in competition with the vast
disgorgements of the past and with one another in the
present. Neither is it at all helpful that books can even
now be reduced to the size of a postage stamp. Avanti!
Place the Bible on a pinhead! Crowding more books into
small spaces does not cram more books into our heads.
Here I come to the sticking point that unnerves the modern
Diphilus. The number of books a person can read in a given
time is, roughly speaking, a historical constant. It does
not change significantly even when the number of books
available for reading does. Constants are pitted against
variables to confound both writer and reader.
Of the following, the MAIN idea in this passage is:
 A. It is difficult to attain immortality because so many books are being published
 B. Too many books are being published, so fewer people are reading them
 C. Because so many books are being published, the quality of the writing is poorer
 D. Because so many books are available, but only a fixed amount of time to read them, frustration results for both the reader and the writer

12. Until recently, consciousness of sexual harassment has   12. ___
been low. But workers have become aware of it as more
women have arrived at levels of authority in the workplace,
feminist groups have focused attention on rape and other
violence against women, and students have felt freer to
report perceived abuse by professors. In the last 5
years, studies have shown that sexual misconduct at the
workplace is a big problem. For example, in a recently
published survey of federal employees, 42% of 694,000
women and 15% of 1,168,000 men said they had experienced
some form of harassment.
According to the author,
 A. the awareness of sexual harassment at the workplace is increasing

B. the incidence of harassment is higher in universities than workplaces
C. sexual harassment is much more commonly experienced by women than men
D. it is rare for men to experience sexual harassment

Questions 13-17.

DIRECTIONS: Questions 13 through 17 are to be answered SOLELY on the basis of the following paragraph.

Since discounts are in common use in the commercial world and apply to purchases made by government agencies as well as business firms, it is essential that individuals in both public and private employment who prepare bills, check invoices, prepare payment vouchers, or write checks to pay bills have an understanding of the terms used. These include cash or time discount, trade discount, and discount series. A cash or time discount offers a reduction in price to the buyer for the prompt payment of the bill and is usually expressed as a percentage with a time requirement, stated in days, within which the bill must be paid in order to earn the discount. An example would be 3/10, meaning a 3% discount may be applied to the bill if the payment is forwarded to the vendor within ten days. On an invoice, the cash discount terms are usually followed by the net terms, which is the time in days allowed for ordinary payment of the bill. Thus, 3/10, Net 30 means that full payment is expected in thirty days if the cash discount of 3% is not taken for having paid the bill within ten days. When the expression Terms Net Cash is listed on a bill, it means that no deduction for early payment is allowed. A trade discount is normally applied to list prices by a manufacturer to show the actual price to retailers so that they may know their cost and determine markups that will allow them to operate competitively and at a profit. A trade discount is applied by the seller to the list price and is independent of a cash or time discount. Discounts may also be used by manufacturers to adjust prices charged to retailers without changing list prices. This is usually done by series discounting and is expressed as a series of percentages. To compute a series discount, such as 40%, 20%, 10%, first apply the 40% discount to the list price, then apply the 20% discount to the remainder, and finally apply the 10% discount to the second remainder.

13. According to the above paragraph, trade discounts are   13.___
    A. applied by the buyer
    B. independent of cash discounts
    C. restricted to cash sales
    D. used to secure rapid payment of bills

14. According to the above paragraph, if the sales terms   14.___
    5/10, Net 60 appear on a bill in the amount of $100
    dated December 5, 1984 and the buyer submits his payment
    on December 15, 1984, his PROPER payment should be
    A. $60   B. $90   C. $95   D. $100

15. According to the above paragraph, if a manufacturer gives   15.___
a trade discount of 40% for an item with a list price of
$250 and the terms are Net Cash, the price a retail mer-
chant is required to pay for this item is
   A. $250   B. $210   C. $150   D. $100

16. According to the above paragraph, a series discount of   16.___
25%, 20%, 10% applied to a list price of $200 results
in an ACTUAL price to the buyer of
   A. $88   B. $90   C. $108   D. $110

17. According to the above paragraph, if a manufacturer gives   17.___
a trade discount of 50% and the terms are 6/10, Net 30,
the cost to a retail merchant of an item with a list price
of $500 and for which he takes the time discount, is
   A. $220   B. $235   C. $240   D. $250

Questions 18-22.

DIRECTIONS: Questions 18 through 22 are to be answered SOLELY on
the basis of the following paragraph.

The city may issue its own bonds or it may purchase bonds as an
investment. Bonds may be issued in various denominations, and the
face value of the bond is its par value. Before purchasing a bond,
the investor desires to know the rate of income that the investment
will yield. In computing the yield on a bond, it is assumed that the
investor will keep the bond until the date of maturity, except for
callable bonds which are not considered in this passage. To compute
exact yield is a complicated mathematical problem, and scientifically
prepared tables are generally used to avoid such computation. However, the approximate yield can be computed much more easily. In
computing approximate yield, the accrued interest on the date of
purchase should be ignored, because the buyer who pays accrued
interest to the seller receives it again at the next interest date.
Bonds bought at a premium (which cost more) yield a lower rate of
income than the same bonds bought at par (face value), and bonds
bought at a discount (which cost less) yield a higher rate of income
than the same bonds bought at par.

18. An investor bought a $10,000 city bond paying 6% interest.   18.___
Which of the following purchase prices would indicate that
the bond was bought at a PREMIUM?
   A. $9,000   B. $9,400   C. $10,000   D. $10,600

19. During 1974, a particular $10,000 bond paying $7\frac{1}{2}$% sold   19.___
at fluctuating prices.
Which of the following prices would indicate that the
bond was bought at a DISCOUNT?
   A. $9,800   B. $10,000   C. $10,200   D. $10,750

20. A certain group of bonds was sold in denominations of   20.___
$5,000, $10,000, $20,000, and $50,000.
In the following list of four purchase prices, which
one is MOST likely to represent a bond sold at par value?
   A. $10,500   B. $20,000   C. $22,000   D. $49,000

21. When computing the approximate yield on a bond, it is DESIRABLE to
    A. assume the bond was purchased at par
    B. consult scientifically prepared tables
    C. ignore accrued interest on the date of purchase
    D. wait until the bond reaches maturity
      21.___

22. Which of the following is MOST likely to be an exception to the information provided in the above paragraph? Bonds
    A. purchased at a premium   B. sold at par
    C. sold before maturity   D. which are callable
      22.___

Questions 23-25.

DIRECTIONS: Questions 23 through 25 are to be answered SOLELY on the basis of the following passage.

There is one bad habit of drivers that often causes chain collisions at traffic lights. It is the habit of keeping one foot poised over the accelerator pedal, ready to step on the gas the instant the light turns green. A driver who is watching the light, instead of watching the cars in front of him, may *jump the gun* and bump the car in front of him, and this car in turn may bump the next car. If a driver is resting his foot on the accelerator, his foot will be slammed down when he bumps into the car ahead. This makes the collision worse and makes it very likely that cars further ahead in the line are going to get involved in a series of violent bumps.

23. Which of the following conclusions can MOST reasonably be drawn from the information given in the above passage?
    A. American drivers have a great many bad driving habits.
    B. Drivers should step on the gas as soon as the light turns green.
    C. A driver with poor driving habits should be arrested and fined.
    D. A driver should not rest his foot on the accelerator when the car is stopped for a traffic light.
      23.___

24. From the information given in the above passage, a reader should be able to tell that a chain collision may be defined as a collision
    A. caused by bad driving habits at traffic lights
    B. in which one car hits another car, this second car hits a third car, and so on
    C. caused by drivers who fail to use their accelerators
    D. that takes place at an intersection where there is a traffic light
      24.___

25. The above passage states that a driver who watches the light instead of paying attention to traffic may
    A. be involved in an accident
    B. end up in jail
    C. lose his license
    D. develop bad driving habits
      25.___

TEST 2

Questions 1-4.

DIRECTIONS: Each of the statements in this section is followed by several labeled choices. In the space at the right, write the letter of the sentence which means MOST NEARLY what is stated or implied in the passage.

1. It may be said that the problem in adult education seems to be not the piling up of facts but practice in thinking. This statement means MOST NEARLY that
   A. educational methods for adults and young people should differ
   B. adults seem to think more than young people
   C. a well-educated adult is one who thinks but does not have a store of information
   D. adult education should stress ability to think

1.____

2. Last year approximately 19,000 fatal accidents were sustained in industry. There were approximately 130 non-fatal injuries to each fatal injury.
   According to the above statement, the number of non-fatal accidents was
   A. 146,000   B. 190,000   C. 1,150,000 D. 2,500,000

2.____

3. No employer expects his stenographer to be a walking encyclopedia, but it is not unreasonable for him to expect her to know where to look for necessary information on a variety of topics.
   The above statement means MOST NEARLY that the stenographer should
   A. be a college graduate
   B. be familiar with standard office reference books
   C. keep a scrapbook of all interesting happenings
   D. go to the library regularly

3.____

4. For the United States, Canada has become the most important country in the world, yet there are few countries about which Americans know less. Canada is the third largest country in the world; only Russia and China are larger. The area of Canada is more than a quarter of the whole British Empire.
   According to the above statement, the
   A. British Empire is smaller than Russia or China
   B. territory of China is greater than that of Canada
   C. Americans know more about Canada than they do about China or Russia
   D. Canadian population is more than one-quarter the population of the British Empire

4.____

10

Questions 5-8.

DIRECTIONS: Questions 5 through 8 are to be answered SOLELY on the
basis of the following paragraph.

A few people who live in old tenements have the bad habit of
throwing garbage out of their windows, especially if there is an
empty lot near their building. Sometimes the garbage is food;
sometimes the garbage is half-empty soda cans. Sometimes the garbage
is a little bit of both mixed together. These people just don't
care about keeping the lot clean.

5. The above paragraph states that throwing garbage out of   5.___
    windows is a
        A. bad habit   B. dangerous thing to do
        C. good thing to do   D. good way to feed rats

6. According to the above paragraph, an empty lot next to an   6.___
    old tenement is sometimes used as a place to
        A. hold local gang meetings B. play ball
        C. throw garbage   D. walk dogs

7. According to the above paragraph, which of the following   7.___
    throw garbage out of their windows?
        A. Nobody   B. Everybody
        C. Most people   D. Some people

8. According to the above paragraph, the kinds of garbage   8.___
    thrown out of windows are
        A. candy and cigarette butts
        B. food and half-empty soda cans
        C. fruit and vegetables
        D. rice and bread

Questions 9-12.

DIRECTIONS: Questions 9 through 12 are to be answered SOLELY on the
basis of the following paragraph.

The game that is recognized all over the world as an all-American
game is the game of baseball. As a matter of fact, baseball heroes
like Joe DiMaggio, Willie Mays, and Babe Ruth were as famous in their
day as movie stars Robert Redford, Paul Newman, and Clint Eastwood
are now. All these men have had the experience of being mobbed by
fans whenever they put in an appearance anywhere in the world. Such
unusual popularity makes it possible for stars like these to earn
at least as much money off the job as on the job. It didn't take
manufacturers and advertising men long to discover that their sales
of shaving lotion, for instance, increased when they got famous stars
to advertise their product for them on radio and television.

9. According to the above paragraph, baseball is known every-   9.___
    where as a(n) _____ game.
        A. all-American   B. fast
        C. unusual   D. tough

11

10. According to the above paragraph, being so well known   10.___
means that it is possible for people like Willie Mays
and Babe Ruth to
    A. ask for anything and get it
    B. make as much money off the job as on it
    C. travel anywhere free of charge
    D. watch any game free of charge

11. According to the above paragraph, which of the following   11.___
are known all over the world?
    A. Baseball heroes   B. Advertising men
    C. Manufacturers   D. Basketball heroes

12. According to the above paragraph, it is possible to sell   12.___
much more shaving lotion on television and radio if
    A. the commercials are in color instead of black and white
    B. you can get a prize with each bottle of shaving lotion
    C. the shaving lotion makes you smell nicer than usual
    D. the shaving lotion is advertisied by famous stars

Questions 13-15.

DIRECTIONS: Questions 13 through 15 are to be answered SOLELY on
the basis of the following passage.

That music gives pleasure is axiomatic. Because this is so, the
pleasures of music may seem a rather elementary subject for discussion.
Yet the source of that pleasure, our musical instinct, is not at all
elementary. It is, in fact, one of the prime puzzles of consciousness.
Why is it that we are able to make sense out of these nerve
signals so that we emerge from engulfment in the orderly presentation
of sound stimuli as if we had lived through an image of life?

If music has impact for the mere listener, it follows that it
will have much greater impact for those who sing it or play it themselves with proficiency. Any educated person in Elizabethan times
was expected to read musical notation and take part in a madrigal-
sing. Passive listeners, numbered in the millions, are a comparative-
ly recent innovation.

Everyone is aware that so-called serious music has made great
strides in general public acceptance in recent years, but the term
itself still connotes something forbidding and hermetic to the mass
audience. They attribute to the professional musician a kind of
initiation into secrets that are forever hidden from the outsider.
Nothing could be more misleading. We all listen to music, profes-
sionals, and non-professionals alike in the same sort of way, in a
dumb sort of way, really, because simple or sophisticated music
attracts all of us in the first instance, on the primordial level
of sheer rhythmic and sonic appeal. Musicians are flattered, no
doubt, by the deferential attitude of the layman in regard to what
he imagines to be our secret understanding of music. But in all
honesty, we musicians know that in the main we listen basically as
others do, because music hits us with an immediacy that we recognize
in the reactions of the most simple minded of music listeners.

13. A suitable title for the above passage would be   13.___
    A. HOW TO LISTEN TO MUSIC
    B. LEARNING MUSIC APPRECIATION
    C. THE PLEASURES OF MUSIC
    D. THE WORLD OF THE MUSICIAN

14. The author implies that the passive listener is one who   14.___
    A. cannot read or play music
    B. does not appreciate serious music
    C. does not keep time to the music by hand or toe tapping
    D. will not attend a concert if he has to pay for the
       privilege

15. The author of the above passage is apparently inconsistent   15.___
    when he discusses
    A. the distinction between the listener who pays for the
       privilege and the one who does not
    B. the historical development of musical forms
    C. the pleasures derived from music by the musician
    D. why it is that we listen to music

Questions 16-18.

DIRECTIONS: Questions 16 through 18 are to be answered SOLELY on
             the basis of the following passage.

Who are the clerisy? They are people who like to read books.
The use of a word so unusual, so out of fashion, can only be excused
on the ground that it has no familiar synonym. The word is little
known because what it describes has disappeared, though I do not
believe it is gone forever. The clerisy are those who read for
pleasure, but not for idleness; who read for pasttime, but not to
kill time; who love books, but do not live by books.

Let us consider the actual business of reading -- the interpre-
tative act of getting the words off the page and into your head in
the most effective way. The most effective way is not the quickest
way of reading; and for those who think that speed is the greatest
good, there are plenty of manuals on how to read a book which profess
to tell how to strip off the husk and guzzle the milk, like a chimp
attacking a coconut. Who among today's readers would whisk through
a poem, eyes aflicker, and say that he had read it? The answer to
that last question must unfortunately be: far too many. For reading
is not respected for the art it is.

Doubtless there are philosophical terms for the attitude of mind
of which hasty reading is one manifestation, but here let us call it
end-gaining, for its victims put ends before means; they value not
reading, but having read. In this, the end-gainers make mischief
and spoil all they do; end-gaining is one of the curses of our
nervously tense, intellectually flabby civilization. In reading,
as in all arts, it is the means, and not the end, which gives delight
and brings the true reward. Not straining forward toward the com-
pletion, but the pleasure of every page as it comes, is the secret
of reading. We must desire to read a book, rather than to have read

it. This change in attitude, so simple to describe, is by no means simple to achieve, if one has lived the life of an end-gainer.

16. A suitable title for the above passage would be
    A. READING FOR ENLIGHTENMENT
    B. THE ART OF RAPID READING
    C. THE WELL-EDUCATED READER
    D. VALUES IN READING

16.___

17. The author does NOT believe that most people read because they
    A. are bored
    B. have nothing better to do
    C. love books
    D. wish to say that they have read certain books

17.___

18. The *change in attitude* to which the author refers in the last sentence of the above passage implies a change from
    A. dawdling while reading so that the reader can read a greater number of books
    B. reading light fiction to reading serious fiction and non-fiction
    C. reading works which do not amuse the reader
    D. skimming through a book to reading it with care

18.___

Questions 19-22.

DIRECTIONS: Questions 19 through 22 are to be answered SOLELY on the basis of the following passage.

Violence is not new to literature. The writings of Shakespeare and Cervantes are full of it. But those classic writers did not condone violence. They viewed it as a just retribution for sins against the divine order or as a sacrifice sanctioned by heroism. What is peculiar to the modern literature is violence for the sake of violence. Perhaps our reverence for life has been dulled by mass slaughter, though mass slaughter has not been exceptional in the history of mankind. What is exceptional is the boredom that now alternates with war. The basic emotion in peacetime has become a horror of emptiness: a fear of being alone, of having nothing to do, a neurosis whose symptoms are restlessness, an unmotivated and undirected rage, sinking at times into vapid listlessness. This neurotic syndrome is intensified by the prevailing sense of insecurity The threat of atomic war has corrupted our faith in life itself.

This universal neurosis has developed with the progress of technology. It is the neurosis of men whose chief expenditure of energy is to pull a lever or push a button, of men who have ceased to make things with their hands. Such inactivity applies not only to muscles and nerves but to the creative processes that once engaged the mind. If one could contrast visually, by time-and-motion studies, the daily actions of an eighteenth-century carpenter with a twentieth-century machinist, the latter would appear as a confined, repetitive clot, the former as a free and even fantastic pattern. But the most significant contrast could not be visualized - the contrast between a mind suspended aimlessly above an autonomous movement and a mind consciously bent on the shaping of a material substance according to the persistent evidence of the senses.

19. A suitable title for the above passage would be
    A. INCREASING PRODUCTION BY MEANS OF SYSTEMATIZATION
    B. LACK OF A SENSE OF CREATIVENESS AND ITS CONSEQUENCE
    C. TECHNOLOGICAL ACHIEVEMENT IN MODERN SOCIETY
    D. WHAT CAN BE DONE ABOUT SENSELESS VIOLENCE

19.____

20. According to the author, Shakespeare treated violence as a
    A. basically sinful act not in keeping with religious thinking
    B. just punishment of transgressors against moral law
    C. means of achieving dramatic excitement
    D. solution to a problem provided no other solution was available

20.____

21. According to the author, boredom may lead to
    A. a greater interest in leisure-time activities
    B. chronic fatigue
    C. senseless anger
    D. the acceptance of a job which does not provide a sense of creativity

21.____

22. The underlined phrase refers to the
    A. hand movements made by the carpenter
    B. hand movements made by the machinist
    C. relative ignorance of the carpenter
    D. relative ignorance of the machinist

22.____

23. The concentration of women and female-headed families in the city is both cause and consequence of the city's fiscal woes. Women live in cities because it is easier and cheaper for them to do so, but because fewer women are employed, and those that are receive lower pay than men, they do not make the same contribution to the tax base that an equivalent population of men would. Concomitantly, they are more dependent on public resources, such as transportation and housing. For these reasons alone, urban finances would be improved by increasing women's employment opportunities and pay. Yet nothing in our current urban policy is specifically geared to improving women's financial resources. There are some proposed incentives to business to create more jobs, but not necessarily ones that would utilize the skills women currently have. The most innovative proposal was a tax credit for new hires from certain groups with particularly high unemployment rates. None of the seven targeted groups were women.
    Which sentence is BEST supported by the above paragraph?
    A. Innovative programs are rapidly improving conditions for seven targeted groups with traditionally high unemployment rates.

23.____

B. The contribution of women to a city's tax base reflects
   their superior economic position.
C. Improving the economic position of women who live in
   cities would help the financial conditions of the
   cities themselves.
D. Most women in this country live in large cities.

24. None of this would be worth saying if Descartes had been   24.___
    right in positing a one-to-one correspondence between
    stimuli and sensations. But we know that nothing of the
    sort exists. The perception of a given color can be evoked
    by an infinite number of differently combined wavelengths.
    Conversely, a given stimulus can evoke a variety of sensa-
    tions, the image of a duck in one recipient, the image of
    a rabbit in another. Nor are responses like these entirely
    innate. One can learn to discriminate colors or patterns
    which were indistinguishable prior to training. To an
    extent still unknown, the production of data from stimuli
    is a learned procedure. After the learning process, the
    same stimulus evokes a different datum. I conclude that,
    though data are the minimal elements of our individual
    experience, they need be shared responses to a given stimu-
    lus only within the membership of a relatively homogeneous
    community: educational, scientific, or linguistic.
    Which sentence is BEST supported by the above paragraph?
    A. One stimulus can give rise to a number of different
       sensations.
    B. There is a one-to-one correspondence between stimuli
       and sensations.
    C. It is not possible to produce data from stimuli by
       using a learned procedure.
    D. It is not necessary for a group to be relatively
       homogeneous in order to share responses to stimuli.

25. Workers who want to move in the direction of participative   25.___
    structures will need to confront the issues of power and
    control. The process of change needs to be mutually shared
    by all involved, or the outcome will not be a really parti-
    cipative model. The demand for a structural redistribution
    of power is not sufficient to address the problem of change
    toward a humanistic, as against a technological, workplace.
    If we are to change our institutional arrangements from
    hierarchy to participation, particularly in our workplaces,
    we will need to look to transformations in ourselves as
    well. As long as we are imbued with the legitimacy of
    hierarchical authority, with the sovereignty of the status
    quo, we will never be able to generate the new and original
    participative forms that we week. This means if we are
    to be equal to the task of reorganizing our workplaces, we
    need to think about how we can reeducate ourselves and
    become aware of our own assumptions about the nature of
    our social life together. Unless the issue is approached
    in terms of these complexities, I fear that all the
    worker participation and quality of work life efforts will
    fail.

According to the above paragraph, which of the following is NOT true?
   A. Self-education concerning social roles must go hand in hand with workplace reorganization.
   B. The structural changing of the workplace, alone, will not bring about the necessary changes in the quality of work life.
   C. Individuals can easily overcome their attitudes towards hierarchical authority.
   D. Changing the quality of work life will require the participation of all involved.

KEY (CORRECT ANSWERS)

TEST 1	TEST 2
1. B	1. D
2. B	2. D
3. B	3. B
4. A	4. B
5. C	5. A
6. B	6. C
7. B	7. D
8. D	8. B
9. D	9. A
10. C	10. B
11. D	11. A
12. A	12. D
13. B	13. C
14. C	14. A
15. C	15. C
16. C	16. D
17. B	17. C
18. D	18. D
19. A	19. B
20. B	20. B
21. C	21. C
22. D	22. B
23. D	23. C
24. B	24. A
25. A	25. C

VERBAL ABILITIES TEST

FORM A

DIRECTIONS AND SAMPLE QUESTIONS

Study the sample questions carefully. Each question has four suggested answers. Decide which one is the best answer. Find the question number on the Sample Answer Sheet. Show your answer to the question by darkening completely the space corresponding to the letter that is the same as the letter of your answer. Keep your mark within the space. If you have to erase a mark, be sure to erase it completely. Mark only one answer for each question. Do NOT mark space E for any question.

SAMPLE VERBAL QUESTIONS

I. *Previous* means most nearly
   A) abandoned   C) timely
   B) former   D) younger

II. (*Reading*) "Just as the procedure of a collection department must be clear cut and definite, the steps being taken with the sureness of a skilled chess player, so the various paragraphs of a collection letter must show clear organization, giving evidence of a mind that, from the beginning, has had a specific end in view."

The quotation best supports the statement that a collection letter should always
   A) show a spirit of sportsmanship
   B) be divided into several paragraphs
   C) be brief, but courteous
   D) be carefully planned

Decide which sentence is preferable with respect to grammar and usage suitable for a formal letter or report.

III. A) They do not ordinarily present these kind of reports in detail like this.
   B) A report of this kind is not hardly ever given in such detail as this one.
   C) This report is more detailed than what such reports ordinarily are.
   D) A report of this kind is not ordinarily presented in as much detail as this one is.

Find the correct spelling of the word and darken the proper answer space. If no suggested spelling is correct, darken space D.

IV. A) athalete   C) athlete
   B) athelete   D) none of these

V. SPEEDOMETER is related to POINTER as WATCH is related to
   A) case   C) dial
   B) hands   D) numerals

SAMPLE ANSWER SHEET						CORRECT ANSWERS TO SAMPLE QUESTIONS				
	A	B	C	D	E		A	B	C	D	E
I						I		■			
II						II				■	
III						III				■	
IV						IV			■		
V						V		■			

1

EXAMINATION SECTION

Read each question carefully. Select the best answer and darken the proper space on the answer sheet.

1. *Flexible* means most nearly
   A) breakable   C) pliable
   B) flammable   D) weak

2. *Option* means most nearly
   A) use   C) value
   B) choice   D) blame

3. To *verify* means most nearly to
   A) examine   C) confirm
   B) explain   D) guarantee

4. *Indolent* means most nearly
   A) moderate   C) selfish
   B) hopeless   D) lazy

5. *Respiration* means most nearly
   A) recovery   C) pulsation
   B) breathing   D) sweating

6. PLUMBER is related to WRENCH as PAINTER is related to
   A) brush   C) shop
   B) pipe   D) hammer

7. LETTER is related to MESSAGE as PACKAGE is related to
   A) sender   C) insurance
   B) merchandise   D) business

8. FOOD is related to HUNGER as SLEEP is related to
   A) night   C) weariness
   B) dream   D) rest

9. KEY is related to TYPEWRITER as DIAL is related to
   A) sun   C) circle
   B) number   D) telephone

Grammar

10. A) I think that they will promote whoever has the best record.
    B) The firm would have liked to have promoted all employees with good records.
    C) Such of them that have the best records have excellent prospects of promotion.
    D) I feel sure they will give the promotion to whomever has the best record.

11. A) The receptionist must answer courteously the questions of all them callers.
    B) The receptionist must answer courteously the questions what are asked by the callers.
    C) There would have been no trouble if the receptionist had have always answered courteously.
    D) The receptionist should answer courteously the questions of all callers.

Spelling

12. A) collapsible   C) collapseble
    B) collapseable   D) none of these

13. A) ambigeuous   C) ambiguous
    B) ambigeous   D) none of these

14. A) predesessor   C) predecesser
    B) predecesar   D) none of these

15. A) sanctioned   C) sanctionned
    B) sancktioned   D) none of these

Reading

16. "The secretarial profession is a very old one and has increased in importance with the passage of time. In modern times, the vast expansion of business and industry has greatly increased the need and opportunities for secretaries, and for the first time in history their number has become large."

    The quotation best supports the statement that the secretarial profession
    A) is older than business and industry
    B) did not exist in ancient times
    C) has greatly increased in size
    D) demands higher training than it did formerly

17. "Civilization started to move ahead more rapidly when man freed himself of the shackles that restricted his search for the truth."

    The quotation best supports the statement that the progress of civilization
    A) came as a result of man's dislike for obstacles
    B) did not begin until restrictions on learning were removed
    C) has been aided by man's efforts to find the truth
    D) is based on continually increasing efforts

GO ON TO SIMILAR QUESTIONS ON NEXT PAGE.

18. *Vigilant* means most nearly
A) sensible
B) watchful
C) suspicious
D) restless

19. *Incidental* means most nearly
A) independent
B) needless
C) infrequent
D) casual

20. *Conciliatory* means most nearly
A) pacific
B) contentious
C) obligatory
D) offensive

21. *Altercation* means most nearly
A) defeat
B) concurrence
C) controversy
D) vexation

22. *Irresolute* means most nearly
A) wavering
B) insubordinate
C) impudent
D) unobservant

23. DARKNESS is related to SUNLIGHT as STILLNESS is related to
A) quiet
B) moonlight
C) sound
D) dark

24. DESIGNED is related to INTENTION as ACCIDENTAL is related to
A) purpose
B) caution
C) damage
D) chance

25. ERROR is related to PRACTICE as SOUND is related to
A) deafness
B) noise
C) muffler
D) horn

26. RESEARCH is related to FINDINGS as TRAINING is related to
A) skill
B) tests
C) supervision
D) teaching

27. A) If properly addressed, the letter will reach my mother and I.
B) The letter had been addressed to myself and my mother.
C) I believe the letter was addressed to either my mother or I.
D) My mother's name, as well as mine, was on the letter.

28. A) The supervisor reprimanded the typist, whom she believed had made careless errors.
B) The typist would have corrected the errors had she of known that the supervisor would see the report.
C) The errors in the typed report were so numerous that they could hardly be overlooked.
D) Many errors were found in the report which she typed and could not disregard them.

29. A) minieture
B) minneature
C) mineature
D) none of these

30. A) extemporaneous
B) extempuraneus
C) extemperaneous
D) none of these

31. A) problemmatical
B) problematical
C) problematicle
D) none of these

32. A) descendant
B) decendant
C) desendant
D) none of these

33. "The likelihood of America's exhausting her natural resources seems to be growing less. All kinds of waste are being re-worked and new uses are constantly being found for almost everything. We are getting more use out of our goods and are making many new byproducts out of what was formerly thrown away."
The quotation best supports the statement that we seem to be in less danger of exhausting our resources because
A) economy is found to lie in the use of substitutes
B) more service is obtained from a given amount of material
C) we are allowing time for nature to restore them
D) supply and demand are better controlled

34. "Telegrams should be clear, concise, and brief. Omit all unnecessary words. The parts of speech most often used in telegrams are nouns, verbs, adjectives, and adverbs. If possible, do without pronouns, prepositions, articles, and copulative verbs. Use simple sentences, rather than complex or compound ones."
The quotation best supports the statement that in writing telegrams one should always use
A) common and simple words
B) only nouns, verbs, adjectives, and adverbs
C) incomplete sentences
D) only the words essential to the meaning

GO ON TO SIMILAR QUESTIONS ON NEXT PAGE.

35. To *counteract* means most nearly to
   A) undermine   C) preserve
   B) censure   D) neutralize

36. *Deferred* means most nearly
   A) reversed   C) considered
   B) delayed   D) forbidden

37. *Feasible* means most nearly
   A) capable   C) practicable
   B) justifiable   D) beneficial

38. To *encounter* means most nearly to
   A) meet   C) overcome
   B) recall   D) retreat

39. *Innate* means most nearly
   A) eternal   C) native
   B) well-developed   D) prospective

40. STUDENT is related to TEACHER as DISCIPLE is related to
   A) follower   C) principal
   B) master   D) pupil

41. LECTURE is related to AUDITORIUM as EXPERIMENT is related to
   A) scientist   C) laboratory
   B) chemistry   D) discovery

42. BODY is related to FOOD as ENGINE is related to
   A) wheels   C) motion
   B) fuel   D) smoke

43. SCHOOL is related to EDUCATION as THEATER is related to
   A) management   C) recreation
   B) stage   D) preparation

44. A) Most all these statements have been supported by persons who are reliable and can be depended upon.
   B) The persons which have guaranteed these statements are reliable.
   C) Reliable persons guarantee the facts with regards to the truth of these statements.
   D) These statements can be depended on, for their truth has been guaranteed by reliable persons.

45. A) The success of the book pleased both his publisher and he.
   B) Both his publisher and he was pleased with the success of the book.
   C) Neither he or his publisher was disappointed with the success of the book.
   D) His publisher was as pleased as he with the success of the book.

46. A) extercate   C) extricate
   B) extracate   D) none of these

47. A) hereditory   C) hereditairy
   B) hereditary   D) none of these

48. A) auspiceous   C) auspicious
   B) auspiseous   D) none of these

49. A) sequance   C) sequense
   B) sequence   D) none of these

50. "The prevention of accidents makes it necessary not only that safety devices be used to guard exposed machinery but also that mechanics be instructed in safety rules which they must follow for their own protection, and that the lighting in the plant be adequate."

The quotation best supports the statement that industrial accidents
   A) may be due to ignorance
   B) are always avoidable
   C) usually result from inadequate machinery
   D) cannot be entirely overcome

51. "The English language is peculiarly rich in synonyms, and there is scarcely a language spoken among men that has not some representative in English speech. The spirit of the Anglo-Saxon race has subjugated these various elements to one idiom, making not a patchwork, but a composite language."

The quotation best supports the statement that the English language
   A) has few idiomatic expressions
   B) is difficult to translate
   C) is used universally
   D) has absorbed words from other languages

GO ON TO SIMILAR QUESTIONS ON NEXT PAGE.

52. To *acquiesce* means most nearly to
   A) assent
   B) acquire
   C) complete
   D) participate

53. *Unanimity* means most nearly
   A) emphasis
   B) namelessness
   C) harmony
   D) impartiality

54. *Precedent* means most nearly
   A) example
   B) theory
   C) law
   D) conformity

55. *Versatile* means most nearly
   A) broad-minded
   B) well-known
   C) up-to-date
   D) many-sided

56. *Authentic* means most nearly
   A) detailed
   B) reliable
   C) valuable
   D) practical

57. BIOGRAPHY is related to FACT as NOVEL is related to
   A) fiction
   B) literature
   C) narration
   D) book

58. COPY is related to CARBON PAPER as MOTION PICTURE is related to
   A) theater
   B) film
   C) duplicate
   D) television

59. EFFICIENCY is related to REWARD as CARELESSNESS is related to
   A) improvement
   B) disobedience
   C) reprimand
   D) repetition

60. ABUNDANT is related to CHEAP as SCARCE is related to
   A) ample
   B) costly
   C) inexpensive
   D) unobtainable

61. A) Brown's & Company employees have recently received increases in salary.
   B) Brown & Company recently increased the salaries of all its employees.
   C) Recently Brown & Company has increased their employees' salaries.
   D) Brown & Company have recently increased the salaries of all its employees.

62. A) In reviewing the typists' work reports, the job analyst found records of unusual typing speeds.
   B) It says in the job analyst's report that some employees type with great speed.
   C) The job analyst found that, in reviewing the typists' work reports, that some unusual typing speeds had been made.
   D) In the reports of typists' speeds, the job analyst found some records that are kind of unusual.

63. A) oblitorate
   B) oblitterat
   C) obbliterate
   D) none of these

64. A) diagnoesis
   B) diagnossis
   C) diagnosis
   D) none of these

65. A) contenance
   B) countenance
   C) countinance
   D) none of these

66. A) conceivably
   B) concieveably
   C) conceiveably
   D) none of these

67. "Through advertising, manufacturers exercise a high degree of control over consumers' desires. However, the manufacturer assumes enormous risks in attempting to predict what consumers will want and in producing goods in quantity and distributing them in advance of final selection by the consumers."

   The quotation best supports the statement that manufacturers
   A) can eliminate the risk of overproduction by advertising
   B) distribute goods directly to the consumers
   C) must depend upon the final consumers for the success of their undertakings
   D) can predict with great accuracy the success of any product they put on the market

68. "In the relations of man to nature, the procuring of food and shelter is fundamental. With the migration of man to various climates, ever new adjustments to the food supply and to the climate became necessary."

   The quotation best supports the statement that the means by which man supplies his material needs are
   A) accidental
   B) varied
   C) limited
   D) inadequate

GO ON TO SIMILAR QUESTIONS ON NEXT PAGE.

69. *Strident* means most nearly
A) swaggering   C) angry
B) domineering   D) harsh

70. To *confine* means most nearly to
A) hide   C) eliminate
B) restrict   D) punish

71. To *accentuate* means most nearly to
A) modify   C) sustain
B) hasten   D) intensify

72. *Banal* means most nearly
A) commonplace   C) tranquil
B) forceful   D) indifferent

73. *Incorrigible* means most nearly
A) intolerable   C) irreformable
B) retarded   D) brazen

74. POLICEMAN is related to ORDER as DOCTOR is related to
A) physician   C) sickness
B) hospital   D) health

75. ARTIST is related to EASEL as WEAVER is related to
A) loom   C) threads
B) cloth   D) spinner

76. CROWD is related to PERSONS as FLEET is related to
A) expedition   C) navy
B) officers   D) ships

77. CALENDAR is related to DATE as MAP is related to
A) geography   C) mileage
B) trip   D) vacation

78. A) Since the report lacked the needed information, it was of no use to him.
B) This report was useless to him because there were no needed information in it.
C) Since the report did not contain the needed information, it was not real useful to him.
D) Being that the report lacked the needed information, he could not use it.

79. A) The company had hardly declared the dividend till the notices were prepared for mailing.
B) They had no sooner declared the dividend when they sent the notices to the stockholders.
C) No sooner had the dividend been declared than the notices were prepared for mailing.
D) Scarcely had the dividend been declared than the notices were sent out.

80. A) compitition   C) competetion
B) competition   D) none of these

81. A) occassion   C) ocassion
B) occasion   D) none of these

82. A) knowlege   C) knowledge
B) knolledge   D) none of these

83. A) deliborate   C) delibrate
B) deliberate   D) none of these

84. "What constitutes skill in any line of work is not always easy to determine; economy of time must be carefully distinguished from economy of energy, as the quickest method may require the greatest expenditure of muscular effort, and may not be essential or at all desirable."

The quotation best supports the statement that
A) the most efficiently executed task is not always the one done in the shortest time
B) energy and time cannot both be conserved in performing a single task
C) a task is well done when it is performed in the shortest time
D) skill in performing a task should not be acquired at the expense of time

85. "It is difficult to distinguish between bookkeeping and accounting. In attempts to do so, bookkeeping is called the art, and accounting the science, of recording business transactions. Bookkeeping gives the history of the business in a systematic manner; and accounting classifies, analyzes, and interprets the facts thus recorded."

The quotation best supports the statement that
A) accounting is less systematic than bookkeeping
B) accounting and bookkeeping are closely related
C) bookkeeping and accounting cannot be distinguished from one another
D) bookkeeping has been superseded by accounting

KEY (CORRECT ANSWERS)

Verbal Test

If the competitor marked more than one answer to any question, draw a line through the answer boxes for the question. To make a stencil, punch out the answers on this page or on a separate answer sheet. Place this punched key over a competitor's sheet. Count the right answers. DO NOT GIVE CREDIT FOR DOUBLE ANSWERS.

Make only ONE mark for each answer. Additional and stray marks may be counted as mistakes. In making corrections, erase errors COMPLETELY.

VERBAL ABILITIES TEST

FORM B

DIRECTIONS AND SAMPLE QUESTIONS

The time allowed both for the sample questions and for the test proper will be announced. Do not turn to page 9 until the signal to do so is given, even though you finish the sample questions.

Use the SPECIAL PENCIL furnished you by the examiner. Fill in the blanks at the top of the ANSWER SHEET. Place no other identifying marks on it. You are to record your answers on the separate answer sheet. For each question, select the best one of the suggested answers. Find the number on the answer sheet that is the same as the number of the question. Then, on the ANSWER SHEET, make a SOLID BLACK MARK in the space between the dotted lines just below the letter that is the same as the letter of your answer. Go over the mark two or three times because your answer sheet will be scored by an electric machine. If you wish to change your answer to a question, be sure to erase your first mark completely (do not merely cross it out) before making another. Make no unnecessary marks on your answer sheet. Keep it on a smooth hard surface.

The questions need not be taken up in order. You may answer first those questions that you are able to answer most readily and then use the remainder of the time for the questions you have omitted.

The sample questions below are similar to the questions in the test proper. Study the sample questions and answer them on the Sample Answer Sheet on the lower right-hand side of this page. Then compare your answers with the Correct Answers for Sample Questions.

SAMPLE QUESTIONS

In each question like samples I and II, select the one of the five suggested answers that means most nearly the same as the word or the group of words that is in italics. Mark the space on the Sample Answer Sheet under the letter that is the same as the letter of the answer you have selected.

  I. To say that information is *authentic* means most nearly that it is
    A) detailed   D) valuable
    B) technical   E) practical
    C) reliable

      The space under C is marked for this question because *reliable* is the one of the five suggested answers that means most nearly the same as *authentic*.

  II. *Previous* means most nearly
    A) abandoned   D) successive
    B) former   E) younger
    C) timely

  III. (*Reading*) "Just as the procedure of a collection department must be clear-cut and definite, the steps being taken with the sureness of a skilled chess player, so the various paragraphs of a collection letter must show clear organization, giving evidence of a mind that, from the beginning, has had a specific end in view."

The quotation best supports the statement that a collection letter should always
  A) show a spirit of sportsmanship
  B) be divided into several paragraphs
  C) express confidence in the debtor
  D) be brief, but courteous
  E) be carefully planned

In each question like the following, find the correct spelling of the word and blacken the proper space on your answer sheet. If no suggested spelling is correct, blacken space D on your answer sheet.

  IV. A) athalete   C) athlete
      B) athelete   D) none of these
    The correct spelling of the word is *athlete*. Since the C spelling is correct, the space under C is marked for this question.

Select the sentence that is preferable with respect to grammar and usage such as would be suitable in a formal letter or report. Then blacken the proper space on the answer sheet.

  V. A) They don't ordinarily present these kind of reports in detail like this.
    B) Reports like this is not generally given in such great detail.
    C) A report of this kind isn't hardly ever given in such detail as this one.
    D) This report is more detailed than what such reports ordinarily are.
    E) A report of this kind is not ordinarily presented in such detail as this one.

SAMPLE ANSWER SHEET						CORRECT ANSWERS FOR SAMPLE QUESTIONS				
	A	B	C	D	E	A	B	C	D	E
I			▮					▮		
II							▮			
III										▮
IV			▮					▮		
V										▮

EXAMINATION SECTION

Read each question carefully. Select the best answer and blacken the proper space on the answer sheet.

1. *Option* means most nearly
   A) use
   B) choice
   C) value
   D) blame
   E) mistake

2. *Irresolute* means most nearly
   A) wavering
   B) insubordinate
   C) impudent
   D) determined
   E) unobservant

3. *Flexible* means most nearly
   A) breakable
   B) inflammable
   C) pliable
   D) weak
   E) impervious

4. To *counteract* means most nearly to
   A) undermine
   B) censure
   C) preserve
   D) sustain
   E) neutralize

5. To *verify* means most nearly to
   A) justify
   B) explain
   C) confirm
   D) guarantee
   E) examine

6. *Indolent* means most nearly
   A) moderate
   B) relentless
   C) selfish
   D) lazy
   E) hopeless

7. To say that an action is *deferred* means most nearly that it is
   A) delayed
   B) reversed
   C) considered
   D) forbidden
   E) followed

8. To *encounter* means most nearly to
   A) meet
   B) recall
   C) overcome
   D) weaken
   E) retreat

9. *Feasible* means most nearly
   A) capable
   B) practicable
   C) justifiable
   D) beneficial
   E) reliable

10. *Respiration* means most nearly
    A) dehydration
    B) breathing
    C) pulsation
    D) sweating
    E) recovery

11. *Vigilant* means most nearly
    A) sensible
    B) ambitious
    C) watchful
    D) suspicious
    E) restless

12. To say that an action is taken *before the proper time* means most nearly that it is taken
    A) prematurely
    B) furtively
    C) temporarily
    D) punctually
    E) presently

13. *Innate* means most nearly
    A) eternal
    B) learned
    C) native
    D) prospective
    E) well-developed

14. *Precedent* means most nearly
    A) duplicate
    B) theory
    C) law
    D) conformity
    E) example

15. To say that the flow of work into an office is *incessant* means most nearly that it is
    A) more than can be handled
    B) uninterrupted
    C) scanty
    D) decreasing in volume
    E) orderly

16. *Unanimity* means most nearly
    A) emphasis
    B) namelessness
    C) disagreement
    D) harmony
    E) impartiality

17. *Incidental* means most nearly
    A) independent
    B) needless
    C) infrequent
    D) necessary
    E) casual

18. *Versatile* means most nearly
    A) broad-minded
    B) well-known
    C) old-fashioned
    D) many-sided
    E) up-to-date

19. *Conciliatory* means most nearly
    A) pacific
    B) contentious
    C) disorderly
    D) obligatory
    E) offensive

20. *Altercation* means most nearly
    A) defeat
    B) concurrence
    C) controversy
    D) consensus
    E) vexation

21. (*Reading*) "The secretarial profession is a very old one and has increased in importance with the passage of time. In modern times, the vast expansion of business and industry has greatly increased the need and opportunities for secretaries, and for the first time in history their number has become large."

    The quotation best supports the statement that the secretarial profession
    A) is older than business and industry
    B) did not exist in ancient times
    C) has greatly increased in size
    D) demands higher training than it did formerly
    E) has always had many members

22. (*Reading*) "The modern system of production unites various kinds of workers into a well-organized body in which each has a definite place."

The quotation best supports the statement that the modern system of production
A) increases production
B) trains workers
C) simplifies tasks
D) combines and places workers
E) combines the various plants

23. (*Reading*) "The prevention of accidents makes it necessary not only that safety devices be used to guard exposed machinery but also that mechanics be instructed in safety rules which they must follow for their own protection, and that the lighting in the plant be adequate."

The quotation best supports the statement that industrial accidents
A) may be due to ignorance
B) are always avoidable
C) usually result from inadequate machinery
D) cannot be entirely overcome
E) result in damage to machinery

24. (*Reading*) "It is wise to choose a duplicating machine that will do the work required with the greatest efficiency and at the least cost. Users with a large volume of business need speedy machines that cost little to operate and are well made."

The quotation best supports the statement that
A) most users of duplicating machines prefer low operating cost to efficiency
B) a well-built machine will outlast a cheap one
C) a duplicating machine is not efficient unless it is sturdy
D) a duplicating machine should be both efficient and economical
E) in duplicating machines speed is more usual than low operating cost

25. (*Reading*) "The likelihood of America's exhausting her natural resources seems to be growing less. All kinds of waste are being reworked and new uses are constantly being found for almost everything. We are getting more use out of our goods and are making many new byproducts out of what was formerly thrown away."

The quotation best supports the statement that we seem to be in less danger of exhausting our resources because
A) economy is found to lie in the use of substitutes
B) more service is obtained from a given amount of material
C) more raw materials are being produced
D) supply and demand are better controlled
E) we are allowing time for nature to restore them

26. (*Reading*) "Probably few people realize, as they drive on a concrete road, that steel is used to keep the surface flat and even, in spite of the weight of busses and trucks. Steel bars, deeply imbedded in the concrete, provide sinews to take the stresses so that they cannot crack the slab or make it wavy."

The quotation best supports the statement that a concrete road
A) is expensive to build
B) usually cracks under heavy weights
C) looks like any other road
D) is used exclusively for heavy traffic
E) is reinforced with other material

27. (*Reading*) "Through advertising, manufacturers exercise a high degree of control over consumers' desires. However, the manufacturer assumes enormous risks in attempting to predict what consumers will want and in producing goods in quantity and distributing them in advance of final selection by the consumers."

The quotation best supports the statement that manufacturers
A) can eliminate the risk of overproduction by advertising
B) completely control buyers' needs and desires
C) must depend upon the final consumers for the success of their undertakings
D) distribute goods directly to the consumers
E) can predict with great accuracy the success of any product they put on the market

28. (*Reading*) "Success in shorthand, like success in any other study, depends upon the interest the student takes in it. In writing shorthand it is not sufficient to know how to write a word correctly; one must also be able to write it quickly."

The quotation best supports the statement that
A) one must be able to read shorthand as well as to write it
B) shorthand requires much study
C) if a student can write correctly, he can also write quickly
D) proficiency in shorthand requires both speed and accuracy
E) interest in shorthand makes study unnecessary

GO ON TO THE NEXT PAGE

10

29. (*Reading*) "The countries in the Western Hemisphere were settled by people who were ready each day for new adventure.. The peoples of North and South America have retained, in addition to expectant and forward-looking attitudes, the ability and the willingness that they have often shown in the past to adapt themselves to new conditions."

The quotation best supports the statement that the peoples in the Western Hemisphere
A) no longer have fresh adventures daily
B) are capable of making changes as new situations arise
C) are no more forward-looking than the peoples of other regions
D) tend to resist regulations
E) differ considerably among themselves

30. (*Reading*) "Civilization started to move ahead more rapidly when man freed himself of the shackles that restricted his search for the truth."

The quotation best supports the statement that the progress of civilization
A) came as a result of man's dislike for obstacles
B) did not begin until restrictions on learning were removed
C) has been aided by man's efforts to find the truth
D) is based on continually increasing efforts
E) continues at a constantly increasing rate

31. (*Reading*) "It is difficult to distinguish between bookkeeping and accounting. In attempts to do so, bookkeeping is called the art, and accounting the science, of recording business transactions. Bookkeeping gives the history of the business in a systematic manner, and accounting classifies, analyzes, and interprets the facts thus recorded."

The quotation best supports the statement that
A) accounting is less systematic than bookkeeping
B) accounting and bookkeeping are closely related
C) bookkeeping and accounting cannot be distinguished from one another
D) bookkeeping has been superseded by accounting
E) the facts recorded by bookkeeping may be interpreted in many ways

32. (*Reading*) "Some specialists are willing to give their services to the Government entirely free of charge; some feel that a nominal salary, such as will cover traveling expenses, is sufficient for a position that is recognized as being somewhat honorary in nature; many other specialists value their time so highly that they will not devote any of it to public service that does not repay them at a rate commensurate with the fees that they can obtain from a good private clientele."

The quotation best supports the statement that the use of specialists by the Government
A) is rare because of the high cost of securing such persons
B) may be influenced by the willingness of specialists to serve
C) enables them to secure higher salaries in private fields
D) has become increasingly common during the past few years
E) always conflicts with private demands for their services

33. (*Reading*) "The leader of an industrial enterprise has two principal functions. He must manufacture and distribute a product at a profit, and he must keep individuals and groups of individuals working effectively together."

The quotation best supports the statement that an industrial leader should be able to
A) increase the distribution of his plant's product
B) introduce large-scale production methods
C) coordinate the activities of his employees
D) profit by the experience of other leaders
E) expand the business rapidly

34. (*Reading*) "The coloration of textile fabrics composed of cotton and wool generally requires two processes, as the process used in dyeing wool is seldom capable of fixing the color upon cotton. The usual method is to immerse the fabric in the requisite baths to dye the wool and then to treat the partially dyed material in the manner found suitable for cotton."

The quotation best supports the statement that the dyeing of textile fabrics composed of cotton and wool
A) is less complicated than the dyeing of wool alone
B) is more successful when the material contains more cotton than wool
C) is not satisfactory when solid colors are desired
D) is restricted to two colors for any one fabric
E) is usually based upon the methods required for dyeing the different materials

11

35. (*Reading*) "The fact must not be overlooked that only about one-half of the international trade of the world crosses the oceans. The other half is merely exchanges of merchandise between countries lying alongside each other or at least within the same continent."

The quotation best supports the statement that
A) the most important part of any country's trade is transoceanic
B) domestic trade is insignificant when compared with foreign trade
C) the exchange of goods between neighboring countries is not considered international trade
D) foreign commerce is not necessarily carried on by water
E) about one-half of the trade of the world is international

36. (*Reading*) "In the relations of man to nature, the procuring of food and shelter is fundamental. With the migration of man to various climates, ever new adjustments to the food supply and to the climate became necessary."

The quotation best supports the statement that the means by which man supplies his material needs are
A) accidental   D) uniform
B) varied   E) inadequate
C) limited

37. (*Reading*) "Every language has its peculiar word associations that have no basis in logic and cannot therefore be reasoned about. These idiomatic expressions are ordinarily acquired only by much reading and conversation although questions about such matters may sometimes be answered by the dictionary. Dictionaries large enough to include quotations from standard authors are especially serviceable in determining questions of idiom."

The quotation best supports the statement that idiomatic expressions
A) give rise to meaningless arguments because they have no logical basis
B) are widely used by recognized authors
C) are explained in most dictionaries
D) are more common in some languages than in others
E) are best learned by observation of the language as actually used

38. (*Reading*) "Individual differences in mental traits assume importance in fitting workers to jobs because such personal characteristics are persistent and are relatively little influenced by training and experience."

The quotation best supports the statement that training and experience
A) are limited in their effectiveness in fitting workers to jobs
B) do not increase a worker's fitness for a job
C) have no effect upon a person's mental traits
D) have relatively little effect upon the individual's chances for success
E) should be based on the mental traits of an individual

39. (*Reading*) "The telegraph networks of the country now constitute wonderfully operated institutions, affording for ordinary use of modern business an important means of communication. The transmission of messages by electricity has reached the goal for which the postal service has long been striving, namely, the elimination of distance as an effective barrier of communication."

The quotation best supports the statement that
A) a new standard of communication has been attained
B) in the telegraph service, messages seldom go astray
C) it is the distance between the parties which creates the need for communication
D) modern business relies more upon the telegraph than upon the mails
E) the telegraph is a form of postal service

40. (*Reading*) "The competition of buyers tends to keep prices up, the competition of sellers to send them down. Normally the pressure of competition among sellers is stronger than that among buyers since the seller has his article to sell and must get rid of it, whereas the buyer is not committed to anything."

The quotation best supports the statement that low prices are caused by
A) buyer competition
B) competition of buyers with sellers
C) fluctuations in demand
D) greater competition among sellers than among buyers
E) more sellers than buyers

GO ON TO THE NEXT PAGE

12

In each question from 41 through 60, find the CORRECT spelling of the word, and blacken the proper space on your answer sheet. Sometimes there is no correct spelling; if none of the suggested spellings is correct, blacken space D on your answer sheet.

41. A) compitition   C) competetion
    B) competition   D) none of these

42. A) diagnoesis   C) diagnosis
    B) diagnossis   D) none of these

43. A) contenance   C) countinance
    B) countenance   D) none of these

44. A) deliborate   C) delibrate
    B) deliberate   D) none of these

45. A) knowlege   C) knowledge
    B) knolledge   D) none of these

46. A) occassion   C) ocassion
    B) occasion   D) none of these

47. A) sanctioned   C) sanctionned
    B) sancktioned   D) none of these

48. A) predesessor   C) predecesser
    B) predecesar   D) none of these

49. A) problemmatical   C) problematicle
    B) problematical   D) none of these

50. A) descendant   C) desendant
    B) decendant   D) none of these

51. A) collapsible   C) collapseble
    B) collapseable   D) none of these

52. A) sequance   C) sequense
    B) sequence   D) none of these

53. A) oblitorate   C) obbliterate
    B) oblitterat   D) none of these

54. A) ambigeuous   C) ambiguous
    B) ambigeous   D) none of these

55. A) minieture   C) mineature
    B) minneature   D) none of these

56. A) extemporaneous   C) extemperaneous
    B) extempuraneus   D) none of these

57. A) hereditory   C) hereditairy
    B) hereditary   D) none of these

58. A) conceivably   C) conceiveably
    B) concieveably   D) none of these

59. A) extercate   C) extricate
    B) extracate   D) none of these

60. A) auspiceous   C) auspicious
    B) auspiseous   D) none of these

Select the sentence that is preferable with respect to grammar and usage such as would be suitable in a formal letter or report. Then blacken the proper space on the answer sheet.

61. A) The receptionist must answer courteously the questions of all them callers.
    B) The questions of all callers had ought to be answered courteously.
    C) The receptionist must answer courteously the questions what are asked by the callers.
    D) There would have been no trouble if the receptionist had have always answered courteously.
    E) The receptionist should answer courteously the questions of all callers.

62. A) I had to learn a great number of rules, causing me to dislike the course.
    B) I disliked that study because it required the learning of numerous rules.
    C) I disliked that course very much, caused by the numerous rules I had to memorize.
    D) The cause of my dislike was on account of the numerous rules I had to learn in that course.
    E) The reason I disliked this study was because there were numerous rules that had to be learned.

63. A) If properly addressed, the letter will reach my mother and I.
    B) The letter had been addressed to myself and mother.
    C) I believe the letter was addressed to either my mother or I.
    D) My mother's name, as well as mine, was on the letter.
    E) If properly addressed, the letter it will reach either my mother or me.

64. A) A knowledge of commercial subjects and a mastery of English are essential if one wishes to be a good secretary.
    B) Two things necessary to a good secretary are that she should speak good English and to know commercial subjects.
    C) One cannot be a good secretary without she knows commercial subjects and English grammar.
    D) Having had good training in commercial subjects, the rules of English grammar should also be followed.
    E) A secretary seldom or ever succeeds without training in English as well as in commercial subjects.

65. A) He suspicions that the service is not so satisfactory as it should be.

B) He believes that we should try and find whether the service is satisfactory.

C) He raises the objection that the way which the service is given is not satisfactory.

D) He believes that the quality of our services are poor.

E) He believes that the service that we are giving is unsatisfactory.

66. A) Most all these statements have been supported by persons who are reliable and can be depended upon.

B) The persons which have guaranteed these statements are reliable.

C) Reliable persons guarantee the facts with regards to the truth of these statements.

D) These statements can be depended on, for their truth has been guaranteed by reliable persons.

E) Persons as reliable as what these are can be depended upon to make accurate statements.

67. A) Brown's & Company's employees have all been given increases in salary.

B) Brown & Company recently increased the salaries of all its employees.

C) Recently Brown & Company has increased their employees' salaries.

D) Brown's & Company employees have recently received increases in salary.

E) Brown & Company have recently increased the salaries of all its employees.

68. A) The personnel office has charge of employment, dismissals, and employee's welfare.

B) Employment, together with dismissals and employees' welfare, are handled by the personnel department.

C) The personnel office takes charge of employment, dismissals, and etc.

D) The personnel office hires and dismisses employees, and their welfare is also its responsibility.

E) The personnel office is responsible for the employment, dismissal, and welfare of employees.

69. A) This kind of pen is some better than that kind.

B) I prefer having these pens than any other.

C) This kind of pen is the most satisfactory for my use.

D) In comparison with that kind of pen, this kind is more preferable.

E) If I were to select between them all, I should pick this pen.

70. A) He could not make use of the report, as it was lacking of the needed information.

B) This report was useless to him because there were no needed information in it.

C) Since the report lacked the needed information, it was of no use to him.

D) Being that the report lacked the needed information, he could not use it.

E) Since the report did not contain the needed information, it was not real useful to him.

71. A) The paper we use for this purpose must be light, glossy, and stand hard usage as well.

B) Only a light and a glossy, but durable, paper must be used for this purpose.

C) For this purpose, we want a paper that is light, glossy, but that will stand hard wear.

D) For this purpose, paper that is light, glossy, and durable is essential.

E) Light and glossy paper, as well as standing hard usage, is necessary for this purpose.

72. A) The company had hardly declared the dividend till the notices were prepared for mailing.

B) They had no sooner declared the dividend when they sent the notices to the stockholders.

C) No sooner had the dividend been declared than the notices were prepared for mailing.

D) Scarcely had the dividend been declared than the notices were sent out.

E) The dividend had not scarcely been declared when the notices were ready for mailing.

GO ON TO THE NEXT PAGE.

14

73. A) Of all the employees, he spends the most time at the office.

B) He spends more time at the office than that of his employees.

C) His working hours are longer or at least equal to those of the other employees.

D) He devotes as much, if not more, time to his work than the rest of the employees.

E) He works the longest of any other employee in the office.

74. A) In the reports of typists' speeds, the job analyst found some records that are kind of unusual.

B) It says in the job analyst's report that some employees type with great speed.

C) The job analyst found that, in reviewing the typists' work reports, that some unusual typing speeds had been made.

D) Work reports showing typing speeds include some typists who are unusual.

E) In reviewing the typists' work reports, the job analyst found records of unusual typing speeds.

75. A) It is quite possible that we shall re-employ anyone whose training fits them to do the work.

B) It is probable that we shall reemploy those who have been trained to do the work.

C) Such of our personnel that have been trained to do the work will be again employed.

D) We expect to reemploy the ones who have had training enough that they can do the work.

E) Some of these people have been trained good and that will determine our re-employing them.

76. A) He as well as his publisher were pleased with the success of the book.

B) The success of the book pleased both his publisher and he.

C) Both his publisher and he was pleased with the success of the book.

D) Neither he or his publisher was disappointed with the success of the book.

E) His publisher was as pleased as he with the success of the book.

77. A) You have got to get rid of some of these people if you expect to have the quality of the work improve.

B) The quality of the work would improve if they would leave fewer people do it.

C) I believe it would be desirable to have fewer persons doing this work.

D) If you had planned on employing fewer people than this to do the work, this situation would not have arose.

E) Seeing how you have all those people on that work, it is not surprising that you have a great deal of confusion.

78. A) She made lots of errors in her typed report, and which caused her to be reprimanded.

B) The supervisor reprimanded the typist, whom she believed had made careless errors.

C) Many errors were found in the report which she typed and could not disregard them.

D) The typist would have corrected the errors, had she of known that the supervisor would see the report.

E) The errors in the typed report were so numerous that they could hardly be overlooked.

79. A) This kind of a worker achieves success through patience.

B) Success does not often come to men of this type except they who are patient.

C) Because they are patient, these sort of workers usually achieve success.

D) This worker has more patience than any man in his office.

E) This kind of worker achieves success through patience.

80. A) I think that they will promote whoever has the best record.

B) The firm would have liked to have promoted all employees with good records.

C) Such of them that have the best records have excellent prospects of promotion.

D) I feel sure they will give the promotion to whomever has the best record.

E) Whoever they find to have the best record will, I think, be promoted.

15

FORM B
KEY (CORRECT ANSWERS)

If the competitor marked more than one answer to any question, draw a line through the answer boxes for the question. To make a stencil, punch out the answers on this page or on a separate answer sheet. Place this punched key over a competitor's sheet. Count the right answers. DO NOT GIVE CREDIT FOR DOUBLE ANSWERS.

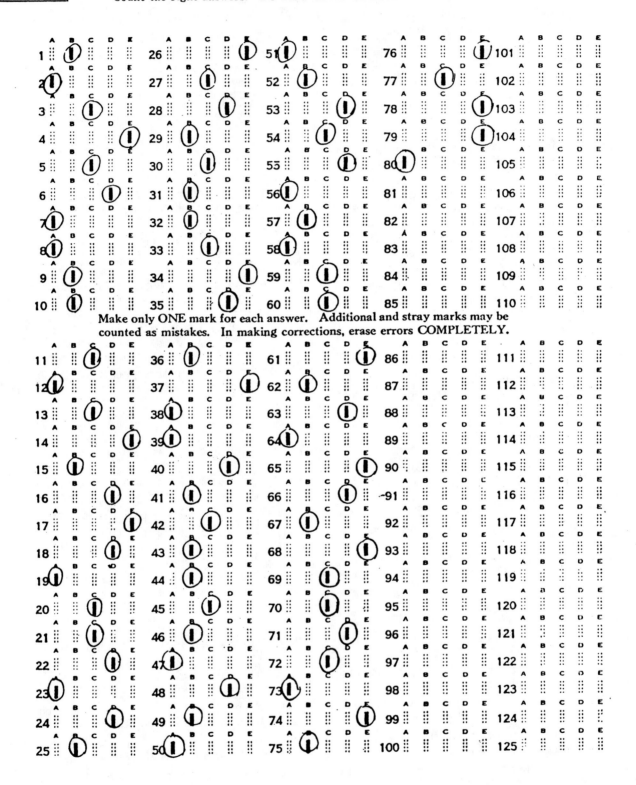

Make only ONE mark for each answer. Additional and stray marks may be counted as mistakes. In making corrections, erase errors COMPLETELY.

EXAMINATION SECTION

DIRECTIONS: Each question or incomplete statement is followed by several suggested answers or completions. Select the one that BEST answers the question or completes the statement. *PRINT THE LETTER OF THE CORRECT ANSWER IN THE SPACE AT THE RIGHT.*

Questions 1-22.

DIRECTIONS: Read through each group of words. Indicate in the space at the right the letter of the misspelled word.

1. A. miniature   B. recession   1.____
    C. accommodate   D. supress

2. A. mortgage   B. illogical   2.____
    C. fasinate   D. pronounce

3. A. calendar   B. heros   3.____
    C. ecstasy   D. librarian

4. A. initiative   B. extraordinary   4.____
    C. villian   D. exaggerate

5. A. absence   B. sense   5.____
    C. dosn't   D. height

6. A. curiosity   B. ninety   6.____
    C. truely   D. grammar

7. A. amateur   B. definate   7.____
    C. meant   D. changeable

8. A. excellent   B. studioes   8.____
    C. achievement   D. weird

9. A. goverment   B. description   9.____
    C. sergeant   D. desirable

10. A. proceed   B. anxious   10.____
    C. neice   D. precede

11. A. environment   B. omitted   11.____
    C. apparant   D. misconstrue

12. A. comparative   B. hindrance   12.____
    C. benefited   D. unamimous

13. A. embarrass   B. recommend   13.____
    C. desciple   D. argument

14. A. sophomore   B. superintendent   14.____
    C. concievable   D. disastrous

15. A. agressive   B. questionnaire   15.____
    C. occurred   D. rhythm

16. A. peaceable   B. conscientious   16.____
    C. redicule   D. deterrent

17. A. mischievious   B. writing   17.____
    C. competition   D. athletics

18. A. auxiliary   B. synonymous   18.____
    C. maneuver   D. repitition

19. A. existence   B. optomistic   19.____
    C. acquitted   D. tragedy

20. A. hypocrisy   B. parrallel   20.____
    C. exhilaration   D. prevalent

21. A. convalesence   B. infallible   21.____
    C. destitute   D. grotesque

22. A. magnanimity   B. asassination   22.____
    C. incorrigible   D. pestilence

Questions 23-40.

DIRECTIONS: In Questions 23 through 40, one sentence contains an
              error in punctuation or capitalization. Indicate the
              letter of the INCORRECT sentence and place it in the
              space at the right.

23. A. Despite a year's work   23.____
    B. in a well-equipped laboratory,
    C. my Uncle failed to complete his research;
    D. now he will never graduate.

24. A. Gene, if you are going to sleep   24.____
    B. all afternoon I will enter
    C. that ladies' golf tournament
    D. sponsored by the Chamber of Commerce.

25. A. Seeing the cat slink toward the barn,   25.____
    B. the farmer's wife jumped off the
    C. ladder picked up a broom, and began
    D. shouting at the top of her voice.

26. A. Extending over southeast Idaho and   26.____
    B. northwest Wyoming, the Tetons
    C. are noted for their height; however the
    D. highest peak is actually under 14,000 feet.

27. A. "Sarah, can you recall the name
     B. of the English queen
     C. who supposedly said, 'We are not
     D. amused?"

27.___

28. A. My aunt's graduation present to me
     B. cost, I imagine more than she could
     C. actually afford. It's a
     D. Swiss watch with numerous features.

28.___

29. A. On the left are examples of buildings
     B. from the Classical Period; two temples
     C. one of which was dedicated to Zeus; the
     D. Agora, a marketplace; and a large arch.

29.___

30. A. Tired of sonic booms, the people who
     B. live near Springfield's Municipal Airport
     C. formed an anti noise organization
     D. with the amusing name of Sound Off.

30.___

31. A. "Joe, Mrs. Sweeney said, "your family
     B. arrives Sunday. Since you'll be in
     C. the Labor Day parade, we could ask Mr.
     D. Krohn, who has a big car, to meet them."

31.___

32. A. The plumber emerged from the basement and
     B. said, "Mr. Cohen I found the trouble in
     C. your water heater. Could you move those
     D. Schwinn bikes out of my way?"

32.___

33. A. The President walked slowly to the
     B. podium, bowed to Edward Everett Hale
     C. the other speaker, and began his formal address:
     D. "Fourscore and seven years ago...."

33.___

34. A. Mr. Fontana, I hope, will arrive before
     B. the beginning of the ceremonies; however,
     C. if his plane is delayed, I have a substitute
     D. speaker who can be here at a moments' notice.

34.___

35. A. Gladys wedding dress, a satin creation,
     B. lay crumpled on the floor; her veil
     C. torn and streaked, lay nearby. "Jilted!"
     D. shrieked Gladys. She was clearly annoyed.

35.___

36. A. Although it is poor grammar, the word
     B. hopefully has become television's newest
     C. pet expression; I hope (to use the correct
     D. form) that it will soon pass from favor.

36.___

37. A.   Plaza Apartment Hotel   37.___
  B.   103 Tower road
  C.   Hampstead, Iowa 52025
  D.   March 13, 1980

38. A. Circulation Department   38.___
  B. British History Illustrated
  C. 3000 Walnut Street
  D. Boulder Colorado 80302

39. A. Dear Sirs: 39.___
  B. Last spring I ordered a subscription to your
  C. magazine. I had read and enjoyed the May
  D. issue containing the article titled "kings."

40. A. I have not however, received a   40.___
  B. single issue. Will you check this?

  C.   Sincerely,

  D.   Maria Herrera

Questions 41-70.

DIRECTIONS: Questions 41 through 70 represent common grammatical
       concerns: subject-verb agreement, appropriate use of
       pronouns, and appropriate use of verbs. Read each
       sentence and indicate the letter of the grammatically
       CORRECT answer in the space at the right.

41. THE REIVERS, one of William Faulkner's last works, 41.___
  ____ made into a movie starring Steve McQueen.
   A. has been   B. have been
   C. are being.   D. were made

42. He ____ on the ground, his eyes fastened on an ant slowly 42.___
  pushing a morsel of food toward the ant hill.
   A. layed   B. laid   C. had laid   D. lay

43. Nobody in the tri-cities ____ to admit that a flood 43.___
  could be disastrous.
   A. are willing   B. have been willing
   C. is willing   D. were willing

44. "____," the senator asked, "have you convinced to run 44.___
  against the incumbent?"
   A. Who   B. Whom   C. Whomever D. Whomsoever

45. Of all the psychology courses that I took, Statistics 101 45.___
  ____ the most demanding.
   A. was   B. are   C. is   D. were

46. Neither the conductor nor the orchestra members ____   46.____
    the music to be applauded so enthusiastically.
    A. were expecting   B. was expecting
    C. is expected   D. has been expecting

47. The requirements for admission to the Lettermen's Club   47.____
    ____ posted outside the athletic director's office for
    months.
    A. was   B. was being
    C. has been   D. have been

48. Please give me a list of the people ____ to compete in   48.____
    the kayak race.
    A. whom you think have planned
    B. who you think has planned
    C. who you think is planning
    D. who you think are planning

49. I saw Eloise and Abelard earlier today; ____ were riding   49.____
    around in a fancy 1956 MG.
    A. she and him   B. her and him
    C. she and he   D. her and he

50. If you ____ the trunk in the attic, I'll unpack it   50.____
    later today.
    A. can sit   B. are able to sit
    C. can set   D. have sat

51. ____ all of the flour been used, or may I borrow three   51.____
    cups?
    A. Have   B. Has   C. Is   D. Could

52. In exasperation, the cycle shop's owner suggested that   52.____
    ____ there too long.
    A. us boys were   B. we boys were
    C. us boys had been   D. we boys had been

53. Idleness as well as money ____ the root of all evil.   53.____
    A. have been   B. were to have been
    C. is   D. are

54. Only the string players from the quartet - Gregory,   54.____
    Isaac,____ - remained after the concert to answer
    questions.
    A. him, and I   B. he, and I
    C. him, and me   D. he, and me

55. Of all the antiques that ____ for sale, Gertrude chose   55.____
    to buy a stupid glass thimble.
    A. was   B. is
    C. would have   D. were

56. The detective snapped, "Don't confuse me with theories about ____ you believe committed the crime!"
    A. who   B. whom   C. whomever   D. which

56.____

57. ____ when we first called, we might have avoided our present predicament.
    A. The plumber's coming
    B. If the plumber would have come
    C. If the plumber had come
    D. If the plumber was to have come

57.____

58. We thought the sun ____ in the north until we discovered that our compass was defective.
    A. had rose   B. had risen
    C. had rised   D. had raised

58.____

59. Each play of Shakespeare's ____ more than ____ share of memorable characters.
    A. contain; its   B. contains; its
    C. contains; it's   D. contain; their

59.____

60. Our English teacher suggested to ____ seniors that either Tolstoy or Dickens ____ the outstanding novelist of the nineteenth century.
    A. we; was considered   B. we; were considered
    C. us; was considered   D. us; were considered

60.____

61. Sherlock Holmes, together with his great friend and companion Dr. Watson, ____ to aid the woman ____ had stumbled into the room.
    A. has agreed; who   B. have agreed; whom
    C. has agreed; whom   D. have agreed; who

61.____

62. Several of the deer ____ when they spotted my backpack ____ open in the meadow.
    A. was frightened; laying   B. were frightened; lying
    C. were frightened; laying   D. was frightened; lying

62.____

63. After the Scholarship Committee announces ____ selection, hysterics often ____.
    A. it's; occur   B. its; occur
    C. their; occur   D. their; occurs

63.____

64. I ____ the key on the table last night so you and ____ could find it.
    A. layed; her   B. lay; she
    C. laid; she   D. laid; her

64.____

65. Some of the antelope ____ wandered away from the meadow where the rancher ____ the block of salt.
    A. has; sat   B. has; set
    C. have; had set   D. has; sets

65.____

66. Macaroni and cheese ____ best to us (that is, to Andy and ____) when Mother adds extra cheddar cheese.
    A. tastes; I   B. tastes; me
    C. taste; me   D. taste; I

67. Frank said, "It must have been ____ called the phone company.
    A. she who   B. she whom
    C. her who   D. her whom

68. The herd ____ moving restlessly at every bolt of lightning; it was either Ted or ____ who saw the beginning of the stampede.
    A. was; me   B. were; I
    C. was; I   D. have been; me

69. The foreman ____ his lateness by saying that his alarm clock ____ until six minutes before eight.
    A. explains; had not rang
    B. explained; has not rung
    C. has explained; rung
    D. explained; hadn't rung

70. Of all the coaches, Ms. Cox is the only one who ____ that Sherry dives more gracefully than ____.
    A. is always saying; I
    B. is always saying; me
    C. are always saying; I
    D. were always saying; me

Questions 71-90.

DIRECTIONS: Choose the word in Questions 71 through 90 that is MOST opposite in meaning to the italicized word.

71. *fact*
    A. statistic   B. statement
    C. incredible   D. conjecture

72. *stiff*
    A. fastidious   B. babble
    C. supple   D. apprehensive

73. *blunt*
    A. concise   B. tactful
    C. artistic   D. humble

74. *foreign*
    A. pertinent   B. comely
    C. strange   D. scrupulous

75. *anger*
    A. infer   B. pacify   C. taint   D. revile

76. *frank*
    A. earnest   B. reticent   C. post   D. expensive   76.____

77. *secure*
    A. precarious B. acquire   C. moderate   D. frenzied   77.____

78. *petty*
    A. harmonious B. careful   C. forthright D. momentous   78.____

79. *concede*
    A. dispute   B. reciprocate   79.____
    C. subvert   D. propagate

80. *benefit*
    A. liquidation   B. bazaar   80.____
    C. detriment   D. profit

81. *capricious*
    A. preposterous   B. constant   81.____
    C. diabolical   D. careless

82. *boisterous*
    A. devious   B. valiant   C. girlish   D. taciturn   82.____

83. *harmony*
    A. congruence B. discord   C. chagrin   D. melody   83.____

84. *laudable*
    A. auspicious   B. despicable   84.____
    C. acclaimed   D. doubtful

85. *adherent*
    A. partisan   B. stoic   C. renegade   D. recluse   85.____

86. *exuberant*
    A. frail   B. corpulent   C. austere   D. bigot   86.____

87. *spurn*
    A. accede   B. flail   87.____
    C. efface   D. annihilate

88. *spontaneous*
    A. hapless   B. corrosive   88.____
    C. intentional   D. willful

89. *disparage*
    A. abolish   B. exude   C. incriminate D. extol   89.____

90. *timorous*
    A. succinct   B. chaste   90.____
    C. audacious   D. insouciant

———

KEY (CORRECT ANSWERS)

1. D	31. A	61. A
2. C	32. B	62. B
3. B	33. B	63. B
4. C	34. D	64. C
5. C	35. A	65. C
6. C	36. B	66. B
7. B	37. B	67. A
8. B	38. D	68. C
9. A	39. D	69. D
10. C	40. A	70. A
11. C	41. A	71. D
12. D	42. D	72. C
13. C	43. C	73. B
14. C	44. B	74. A
15. A	45. A	75. B
16. C	46. A	76. B
17. A	47. D	77. A
18. D	48. A	78. D
19. B	49. C	79. A
20. B	50. C	80. C
21. A	51. B	81. B
22. B	52. D	82. D
23. C	53. C	83. B
24. B	54. B	84. B
25. C	55. D	85. C
26. C	56. B	86. C
27. Ç	57. C	87. A
28. B	58. B	88. C
29. B	59. B	89. D
30. C	60. C	90. C

WORD MEANING
EXAMINATION SECTION
TEST 1

DIRECTIONS: For the following questions, select the word or group of words lettered A, B, C, D, or E that means MOST NEARLY the same as the word in capital letters. *PRINT THE LETTER OF THE CORRECT ANSWER IN THE SPACE AT THE RIGHT.*

1. ANTIDOTE means *most nearly*   1._____
   A. cure-all   B. diet   C. laxative   D. remedy   E. salve

2. AMICABLE means *most nearly*   2._____
   A. constant   B. friendly   C. pliable   D. tough   E. vigorous

3. To DIVULGE means *most nearly* to   3._____
   A. hide   B. muddle   C. reveal   D. suspect   E. understand

4. PASSIVE means *most nearly*   4._____
   A. helpful   B. impulsive
   C. submissive   D. tired
   E. treacherous

5. DETRIMENTAL means *most nearly*   5._____
   A. determined   B. forceful   C. injurious   D. potent   E. tactful

6. INCOHERENT means *most nearly*   6._____
   A. brief   B. disconnected
   C. exaggerated   D. hasty
   E. inadequate

7. To MASTICATE means *most nearly* to   7._____
   A. assimilate   B. chew   C. digest   D. liberate   E. slice

8. VERTICAL means *most nearly*   8._____
   A. curved   B. direct
   C. flat   D. perpendicular
   E. straight

9. CREDIBLE means *most nearly*   9._____
   A. believable   B. praiseworthy   C. readable
   D. religious   E. understandable

10. VERACITY means *most nearly*   10._____
    A. truth   B. beauty   C. importance   D. luck   E. necessity

KEY (CORRECT ANSWERS)

1.	D	6.	B
2.	B	7.	B
3.	C	8.	D
4.	C	9.	A
5.	C	10.	A

TEST 2

DIRECTIONS: For the following questions, select the word or group of words lettered A, B, C, D, or E that means MOST NEARLY the same as the word in capital letters. *PRINT THE LETTER OF THE CORRECT ANSWER IN THE SPACE AT THE RIGHT.*

1. FICTITIOUS means *most nearly*   1.____

    A. difficult   B. imaginary   C. novel   D. ordinary   E. unknown

2. EPISODE means *most nearly*   2.____

    A. fable   B. incident   C. letter   D. postscript   E. reverie

3. FAMILIAR means *most nearly*   3.____

    A. actual   B. adequate   C. real   D. related   E. well-known

4. METHODICALLY means *most nearly*   4.____

    A. calmly   B. carelessly
    C. openly   D. systematically
    E. vigorously

5. LISTLESS means *most nearly*   5.____

    A. attentive   B. delighted   C. slender   D. languid   E. thoughtful

6. INGENIOUS means *most nearly*   6.____

    A. clever   B. crafty   C. insipid   D. naive   E. sincere

7. To OBSTRUCT means *most nearly* to   7.____

    A. block   B. build   C. disturb   D. experiment   E. imprison

8. HUMANE means *most nearly*   8.____

    A. benevolent   B. convincing   C. traditional   D. virile   E. welcome

9. EMISSARY means *most nearly*   9.____

    A. alien   B. pioneer   C. envoy   D. saboteur   E. substitute

10. INFESTED means *most nearly*   10.____

    A. devoured   B. introduced   C. overrun   D. surrounded   E. tainted

———————

KEY (CORRECT ANSWERS)

1.	B	6.	A
2.	B	7.	A
3.	E	8.	A
4.	D	9.	C
5.	D	10.	C

———

TEST 3

DIRECTIONS: For the following questions, select the word or group of words lettered A, B, C, D, or E that means MOST NEARLY the same as the word in capital letters. *PRINT THE LETTER OF THE CORRECT ANSWER IN THE SPACE AT THE RIGHT.*

1. DILEMMA means *most nearly*   1._____

   A. quarrel   B. denial
   C. predicament   D. apparition
   E. embarrassment

2. APPORTIONED means *most nearly*   2._____

   A. collected   B. saved
   C. changed   D. distributed
   E. accumulated

3. To WRITHE means *most nearly* to   3._____

   A. slip   B. sob   C. relax   D. resist   E. squirm

4. CALLOUS means *most nearly*   4._____

   A. flowerlike   B. harmful   C. pale   D. unfeeling   E. warm

5. MEDIOCRE means *most nearly*   5._____

   A. ordinary   B. confused
   C. skillful   D. distraught
   E. self-satisfied

6. FIDELITY means *most nearly*   6._____

   A. bank   B. loyalty   C. insurance   D. policy   E. valor

7. To MOCK means *most nearly* to   7._____

   A. injure   B. grieve   C. laugh   D. dull   E. taunt

8. MARTIAL means *most nearly*   8._____

   A. warlike   B. married   C. creative   D. unyielding   E. strict

9. To TRANSCEND means *most nearly* to   9._____

   A. translate   B. enjoy   C. strike out   D. surpass   E. climb

10. BOORISH means *most nearly*   10._____

   A. tiresome   B. monotonous
   C. rude   D. argumentative
   E. sporting

KEY (CORRECT ANSWERS)

1. C	6. B
2. D	7. E
3. E	8. A
4. D	9. D
5. A	10. C

———

TEST 4

DIRECTIONS: For the following questions, select the word or group of words lettered A, B, C, D, or E that means MOST NEARLY the same as the word in capital letters. *PRINT THE LETTER OF THE CORRECT ANSWER IN THE SPACE AT THE RIGHT.*

1. To ABRIDGE means *most nearly* to   1.____

    A. dilate   B. shorten   C. go over   D. build   E. connect

2. HUMID means *most nearly*   2.____

    A. funny   B. hot   C. kindly   D. moist   E. normal

3. To STABILIZE means *most nearly* to   3.____

    A. fasten   B. pick   C. steady   D. succor   E. vary

4. PENSIVE means *most nearly*   4.____

    A. awkward   B. declining   C. iridescent   D. thoughtful   E. thwarted

5. To ALLOT means *most nearly* to   5.____

    A. apportion   B. economize   C. offer   D. permit   E. restrict

6. To IMPEACH means *most nearly* to   6.____

    A. accuse   B. convict   C. sear   D. preserve   E. pierce

7. PREDICAMENT means *most nearly*   7.____

    A. argument   B. danger
    C. plight   D. prominence
    E. struggle

8. INFRINGEMENT means *most nearly*   8.____

    A. admission   B. assessment   C. dissolution
    D. restriction   E. violation

9. To SANCTION means *most nearly* to   9.____

    A. condemn   B. destroy   C. neutralize   D. terrify   E. ratify

10. VINDICTIVE means *most nearly*   10.____

    A. colorful   B. helpful   C. sour   D. revengeful   E. winning

KEY (CORRECT ANSWERS)

1.	B		6.	A
2.	D		7.	C
3.	C		8.	E
4.	D		9.	E
5.	A		10.	D

———

TEST 5

DIRECTIONS: For the following questions, select the word or group of words lettered A, B, C, D, or E that means MOST NEARLY the same as the word in capital letters. *PRINT THE LETTER OF THE CORRECT ANSWER IN THE SPACE AT THE RIGHT.*

1. LOYAL means *most nearly*   1.____

   A. unhappy   B. faithful
   C. lazy   D. treacherous
   E. industrious

2. LIBERTY means *most nearly*   2.____

   A. impartiality   B. bondage   C. equality
   D. freedom   E. brotherhood

3. To ADJUST means *most nearly* to   3.____

   A. hold   B. arrange   C. stick   D. upset   E. drop

4. URGENT means *most nearly*   4.____

   A. important   B. simple   C. tedious   D. complicated E. trivial

5. PROSPERITY means *most nearly*   5.____

   A. success   B. indulgence
   C. failure   D. discipline
   E. disappointment

6. SAVAGE means *most nearly*   6.____

   A. cruel   B. friendly   C. gentle   D. opposed   E. snobbish

7. EXPANSION means *most nearly*   7.____

   A. application   B. increase   C. aggression
   D. submission   E. contraction

8. CURIOSITY means *most nearly*   8.____

   A. inquisitiveness   B. indifference   C. impertinence
   D. ignorance   E. knowledge

9. DISTRESS means *most nearly*   9.____

   A. suspicion   B. misery   C. reliance   D. comfort   E. jealousy

10. REALITY means *most nearly*   10.____

   A. fancifulness   B. actuality   C. misunderstanding
   D. conundrum   E. perception

KEY (CORRECT ANSWERS)

1.	B		6.	A
2.	D		7.	B
3.	B		8.	A
4.	A		9.	B
5.	A		10.	B

———

TEST 6

DIRECTIONS: For the following questions, select the word or group of words lettered A, B, C, D, or E that means MOST NEARLY the same as the word in capital letters. *PRINT THE LETTER OF THE CORRECT ANSWER IN THE SPACE AT THE RIGHT.*

1. To OBTAIN means *most nearly* to   1.____

   A. lose   B. risk   C. keep   D. guarantee   E. gain

2. SILENCE means *most nearly*   2.____

   A. confusion   B. leisure   C. noise   D. peace   E. stillness

3. To PROTEST means *most nearly* to   3.____

   A. repeal   B. maintain   C. accede   D. modify   E. object

4. STRANGER means *most nearly*   4.____

   A. acquaintance   B. newcomer
   C. superior   D. ally
   E. enemy

5. To GRATIFY means *most nearly* to   5.____

   A. idolize   B. displease   C. prevent   D. assist   E. delight

6. ODDITY means *most nearly*   6.____

   A. speculation B. industry   C. disgrace   D. peculiarity E. regularity

7. To DALLY means *most nearly* to   7.____

   A. hurry   B. leave   C. lose   D. delay   E. maintain

8. MASSIVE means *most nearly*   8.____

   A. energetic B. heavy   C. peaceful   D. slight   E. dormant

9. KNOLL means *most nearly*   9.____

   A. depression B. portal   C. mound   D. plane   E. exit

10. To BLEND means *most nearly* to   10.____

   A. brighten   B. watch   C. mix   D. darken   E. separate

KEY (CORRECT ANSWERS)

1.	E	6.	D
2.	E	7.	D
3.	E	8.	B
4.	B	9.	C
5.	E	10.	C

———

TEST 7

DIRECTIONS: For the following questions, select the word or group of words lettered A, B, C, D, or E that means MOST NEARLY the same as the word in capital letters. *PRINT THE LETTER OF THE CORRECT ANSWER IN THE SPACE AT THE RIGHT.*

1. INVESTIGATE means *most nearly*　　　　　　　　　　　　　　　　1._____

    A. notify   B. upset   C. search   D. invite   E. envelop

2. ODD means *most nearly*　　　　　　　　　　　　　　　　　　　2._____

    A. antique   B. unknown   C. unusual   D. worn-out   E. worthless

3. POSITIVE means *most nearly*　　　　　　　　　　　　　　　　3._____

    A. sure   B. dependent
    C. neutral   D. contradictory
    E. accurate

4. To COAX means *most nearly* to　　　　　　　　　　　　　　　4._____

    A. urge   B. help   C. compel   D. order   E. mislead

5. To EVAPORATE means *most nearly* to　　　　　　　　　　　　5._____

    A. dry   B. help   C. cook   D. bake   E. spill

6. EVIDENCE means *most nearly*　　　　　　　　　　　　　　　　6._____

    A. inquiry   B. discovery   C. proof   D. explanation E. trial

7. TORRID means *most nearly*　　　　　　　　　　　　　　　　　7._____

    A. warm   B. hot   C. cool   D. damp   E. changeable

8. To REDUCE means most nearly to　　　　　　　　　　　　　　8._____

    A. lessen   B. come back C. oppose   D. smooth out E. prepare

9. To IGNORE means *most nearly* to　　　　　　　　　　　　　　9._____

    A. insult   B. disregard   C. keep out   D. throw away E. disappoint

10. SABOTAGE means *most nearly*　　　　　　　　　　　　　　　10._____

    A. safety first   B. operation   C. protection
    D. destruction   E. alien enemy

KEY (CORRECT ANSWERS)

1.	C		6.	C
2.	C		7.	B
3.	A		8.	A
4.	A		9.	B
5.	A		10.	D

———

TEST 8

DIRECTIONS: For the following questions, select the word or group of words lettered A, B, C, D, or E that means MOST NEARLY the same as the word in capital letters. *PRINT THE LETTER OF THE CORRECT ANSWER IN THE SPACE AT THE RIGHT.*

1. VIOLENT means *most nearly*   1.____

    A. variable   B. persistent   C. furious   D. limited   E. hasty

2. To EXAGGERATE means *most nearly* to   2.____

    A. overstate   B. question   C. annoy   D. estimate   E. argue

3. To FORTIFY means *most nearly* to   3.____

    A. build   B. fight   C. improve   D. strengthen   E. surround

4. CONFLICT means *most nearly*   4.____

    A. meeting   B. settlement   C. struggle   D. flight   E. disorder

5. IMPUDENT means *most nearly*   5.____

    A. angry   B. saucy
    C. friendly   D. uick-tempered
    E. reckless

6. ADMINISTRATION means *most nearly*   6.____

    A. approval   B. assistance   C. property
    D. politics   E. management

7. INTENTION means *most nearly*   7.____

    A. wish   B. purpose
    C. opinion   D. earnestness
    E. anxiety

8. VALOR means *most nearly*   8.____

    A. courage   B. enthusiasm   C. freedom   D. power   E. peril

9. ISOLATION means *most nearly*   9.____

    A. production   B. cooperation   C. absence
    D. opposition   E. separation

10. ZEAL means *most nearly*   10.____

    A. honesty   B. independence
    C. kindness   D. faith
    E. eagerness

KEY (CORRECT ANSWERS)

1.	C	6.	E
2.	A	7.	B
3.	D	8.	A
4.	C	9.	E
5.	B	10.	E

———

WORD MEANING

EXAMINATION SECTION
TEST 1

DIRECTIONS: Each question or incomplete statement is followed by several suggested answers or completions. Select the one that BEST answers the question or completes the statement. *PRINT THE LETTER OF THE CORRECT ANSWER IN THE SPACE AT THE RIGHT.*

1. Local responsibility for the relief of economic need long having been recognized as inadequate, the state and federal governments have established schemes of *categorical* assistance and social insurance.
   In the preceding sentence, the italicized word means MOST NEARLY

   A. conditional
   C. pecuniary
   B. economic
   D. classified

1._____

2. When a person *vicariously* lives out his own problems in novels and plays, he is engaging in an experience that is, in terms of the italicized word in this sentence,

   A. dynamic
   C. substituted
   B. monastic
   D. dignified

2._____

3. The Alcoholics Anonymous program, which in essence amounts to a *therapeutic* procedure, is codified into twelve steps. The italicized word in the preceding sentence means MOST NEARLY

   A. compensatory
   C. sequential
   B. curative
   D. volitional

3._____

4. The professor developed a different central theme during every *semester.*
   The italicized word in the preceding sentence means MOST NEARLY

   A. bi-annual period of instruction
   B. orientation period
   C. slide demonstration
   D. weekly lecture series

4._____

5. To say that the Community Chest movement seems to have been *indigenous* to the North American continent describes this movement, in terms of the italicized word in this sentence, MOST NEARLY as

   A. imported
   C. native
   B. essential
   D. homogeneous

5._____

6. There should be no *opprobrium* attached to the term "second-hand housing" since every house is second-hand after the first occupancy.
   The italicized word in the preceding sentence means MOST NEARLY

   A. stigma   B. honor   C. rank   D. credit

6._____

7. Clinics are now seeing many people who complain of seriously disturbed feelings and other symptoms relating to *traumatic* war experiences.
In the preceding sentence, the italicized word means MOST NEARLY

    A. recent   B. worldwide
    C. prodigious   D. shocking

 7._

8. The nature of the *pathology* underlying the compulsion is obscure.
In the preceding sentence, the italicized word means MOST NEARLY

    A. drive   B. disease
    C. deterioration   D. development

 8._

9. If the interests of a social welfare agency are concerned with bringing opportunities for self-help to underprivileged *ethnic* groups, its activities involve MOST NEARLY, in terms of the italicized word in this sentence,

    A. racial factors   B. minority units
    C. religious affiliations   D. economic conditions

 9._

10. Increased facilities for medical care (though interrupted to some extent by the *exigencies* of wartime) will safeguard the health of many children who in previous generations would have been doomed to an early death or to physical disability.
In the preceding sentence, the MOST NEARLY CORRECT equivalent of the italicized word is

    A. obstacles   B. occurrences
    C. extenuations   D. exactions

 10._

11. He described a hypothetical situation to illustrate his point.
In the preceding sentence, the word *hypothetical* means MOST NEARLY

    A. actual   B. theoretical
    C. typical   D. unusual

 11._

12. I gave tacit approval to my partner's proposed business changes.
In the preceding sentence, the word *tacit* means MOST NEARLY

    A. enthusiastic   B. partial
    C. silent   D. written

 12._

13. Jones was considered an astute lawyer by the members of his profession.
In the preceding sentence, the word *astute* means MOST NEARLY

    A. clever   B. persevering
    C. poorly trained   D. unethical

 13._

14. There were intimations even in early days of the way in which he would go.
In the preceding sentence, the word *intimations* means MOST NEARLY

    A. hints   B. patterns   C. plans   D. purposes

 14._

15. His last book was published posthumously.
In the preceding sentence, the word *posthumously* means MOST NEARLY

    A. after the death of the author
    B. printed free by the publisher
    C. without a dedication
    D. without royalties

 15._

16. When he was challenged, he used every known subterfuge. In the preceding sentence, the word *subterfuge* means MOST NEARLY

    16.____

    A. evasion to justify one's conduct
    B. means of attack to defend one's self
    C. medical device
    D. unconscious thought

17. His partner suggested a course of action that would alleviate the difficulties which confronted him.
In the preceding sentence, the word *alleviate* means MOST NEARLY

    17.____

    A. correct   B. lessen   C. remove   D. solve

18. Among the applicants for the new apartment, white collar workers were preponderant.
In the preceding sentence, the word *preponderant* means MOST NEARLY

    18.____

    A. considered not eligible   B. in evidence
    C. superior in number   D. the first to apply

19. The captain gave a lucid explanation of his plans for the coming campaign.
In the preceding sentence, the word *lucid* means MOST NEARLY

    19.____

    A. clear   B. graphic
    C. interesting   D. thorough

20. He led a sedentary life.
In the preceding sentence, the word *sedentary* means MOST NEARLY

    20.____

    A. aimless   B. exciting   C. full   D. inactive

21. His plan for the next campaign was very plausible.
In the preceding sentence, the word *plausible* means MOST NEARLY

    21.____

    A. appropriate   B. believable
    C. usable   D. valuable

22. The office manager thought it advisable to mollify his subordinate.
The word *mollify,* as used in this sentence, means MOST NEARLY

    22.____

    A. reprimand   B. caution   C. calm   D. question

23. The bureau chief adopted a dilatory policy.
The word *dilatory,* as used in this sentence, means MOST NEARLY

    23.____

    A. tending to cause delay
    B. acceptable to all affected
    C. severe but fair
    D. prepared with great care

24. He complained about the paucity of requests.
The word *paucity,* as used in this sentence, means MOST NEARLY

    24.____

    A. great variety   B. unreasonableness
    C. unexpected increase   D. scarcity

25. To say that an event is *imminent* means MOST NEARLY that it is

    A. near at hand   B. unpredictable
    C. favorable or happy   D. very significant

26. The general manager delivered a laudatory speech.
The word *laudatory,* as used in this sentence, means MOST NEARLY

    A. clear and emphatic   B. lengthy
    C. introductory   D. expressing praise

27. We all knew of his aversion for performing statistical work.
The word *aversion,* as used in this sentence, means MOST NEARLY

    A. training   B. dislike
    C. incentive   D. lack of preparation

28. The engineer was circumspect in making his recommendations.
The word *circumspect,* as used in this sentence, means MOST NEARLY

    A. hostile   B. outspoken   C. biased   D. cautious

29. To say that certain clerical operations were *obviated* means MOST NEARLY that these operations were

    A. extremely distasteful   B. easily understood
    C. made unnecessary   D. very complicated

30. The interviewer was impressed with the client's demeanor. The word *demeanor,* as used in this sentence, means MOST NEARLY

    A. outward manner   B. plan of action
    C. fluent speech   D. extensive knowledge

31. To say that the information was *gratuitous* means MOST NEARLY that it was

    A. given freely   B. deeply appreciated
    C. brief   D. valuable

32. She considered the supervisor's action to be arbitrary. The word *arbitrary,* as used in this sentence, means MOST NEARLY

    A. inconsistent   B. justifiable
    C. appeasing   D. dictatorial

33. He sent the irate employee to the personnel manager. The word *irate* means MOST NEARLY

    A. irresponsible   B. untidy
    C. insubordinate   D. angry

34. An *ambiguous* statement is one which is

    A. forceful and convincing
    B. capable of being understood in more than one sense
    C. based upon good judgment and sound reasoning processes
    D. uninteresting and too lengthy

35. To *extol* means MOST NEARLY to   35.____

    A. summon   B. praise   C. reject   D. withdraw

36. The word *proximity* means MOST NEARLY   36.____

    A. similarity   B. exactness
    C. harmony   D. nearness

37. His friends had a detrimental influence on him.   37.____
    The word *detrimental* means MOST NEARLY

    A. favorable   B. lasting
    C. harmful   D. short-lived

38. The chief inspector relied upon the veracity of his inspectors.   38.____
    The word *veracity* means MOST NEARLY

    A. speed   B. assistance
    C. shrewdness   D. truthfulness

39. There was much diversity in the suggestions submitted.   39.____
    The word *diversity* means MOST NEARLY

    A. similarity   B. value
    C. triviality   D. variety

40. The survey was concerned with the problem of indigence.   40.____
    The word *indigence* means MOST NEARLY

    A. poverty   B. corruption
    C. intolerance   D. morale

41. The investigator considered this evidence to be extraneous.   41.____
    The word *extraneous* means MOST NEARLY

    A. significant   B. pertinent but unobtainable
    C. not essential   D. inadequate

42. He was surprised at the temerity of the new employee.   42.____
    The word *temerity* means MOST NEARLY

    A. shyness   B. enthusiasm
    C. rashness   D. self-control

43. The term *ex officio* means MOST NEARLY   43.____

    A. expelled from office
    B. a former holder of a high office
    C. without official approval
    D. by virtue of office or position

44. The aims of the students and the aims of the faculty often coincide.   44.____
    The word *coincide* means MOST NEARLY

    A. agree   B. are ignored
    C. conflict   D. are misinterpreted

45. The secretary of the department was responsible for setting up an index of relevant mag-   45._
azine articles.
The word *relevant* means MOST NEARLY

   A. applicable   B. controversial
   C. miscellaneous   D. recent

46. One of the secretary's duties consisted of sorting and filing facsimiles of student term   46._
papers.
The word *facsimiles* means MOST NEARLY

   A. bibliographical listings
   B. exact copies
   C. summaries
   D. supporting documentation

47. Stringent requirements for advanced physics courses often result in small class sizes.   47._
The word *stringent* means MOST NEARLY

   A. lengthy   B. remarkable
   C. rigid   D. vague

48. The professor explained that the report was too verbose to be submitted.   48._
The word *verbose* means MOST NEARLY

   A. brief   B. specific   C. general   D. wordy

49. The faculty meeting pre-empted the conference room in the Dean's office.   49._
The word *pre-empted* means MOST NEARLY

   A. appropriated   B. emptied
   C. filled   D. reserved

50. The professor's credentials became a subject of controversy.   50._
The word *controversy* means MOST NEARLY

   A. annoyance   B. debate   C. envy   D. review

KEY (CORRECT ANSWERS)

1. D	11. B	21. B	31. A	41. C
2. C	12. C	22. C	32. D	42. C
3. B	13. A	23. A	33. D	43. D
4. A	14. A	24. D	34. B	44. A
5. C	15. A	25. A	35. B	45. A
6. A	16. A	26. D	36. D	46. B
7. D	17. B	27. B	37. C	47. C
8. B	18. C	28. D	38. D	48. D
9. A	19. A	29. C	39. D	49. A
10. D	20. D	30. A	40. A	50. B

TEST 2

DIRECTIONS: Each question or incomplete statement is followed by several suggested answers or completions. Select the one that BEST answers the question or completes the statement. *PRINT THE LETTER OF THE CORRECT ANSWER IN THE SPACE AT THE RIGHT.*

1. The suspect was detained until a witness proved he could not have committed the crime.
   As used in this sentence, the word *detained* means MOST NEARLY

   A. suspected   B. accused   C. held   D. observed

   1.____

2. The fireman's equilibrium improved shortly after he had stumbled out of the smoke-filled building.
   As used in this sentence, the word *equilibrium* means MOST NEARLY

   A. breathing   B. balance   C. vision   D. vigor

   2.____

3. The water supply in the tank began to dwindle soon after the pumps were turned on.
   As used in this sentence, the word *dwindle* means MOST NEARLY

   A. grow smaller   B. whirl about
   C. become muddy   D. overflow

   3.____

4. They thought his illness was feigned.
   As used in this sentence, the word *feigned* means MOST NEARLY

   A. hereditary   B. contagious
   C. pretended   D. incurable

   4.____

5. The officer corroborated the information given by the fireman.
   As used in this sentence, the word *corroborated* means MOST NEARLY

   A. questioned   B. confirmed
   C. corrected   D. accepted

   5.____

6. Only after an inspection were they even able to surmise what caused the fire.
   As used in this sentence, the word *surmise* means MOST NEARLY

   A. guess   B. discover   C. prove   D. isolate

   6.____

7. Officers shall report all flagrant violations of regulations or laws by subordinates.
   As used in this sentence, the word *flagrant* means MOST NEARLY

   A. glaring   B. accidental
   C. habitual   D. minor

   7.____

8. The man was cajoled into signing the contract.
   As used in this sentence, the word *cajoled* means MOST NEARLY

   A. bribed   B. coaxed   C. confused   D. forced

   8.____

9. The announcement was met with general derision.
   As used in this sentence, the word *derision* means MOST NEARLY

   A. anger   B. applause   C. disbelief   D. ridicule

   9.____

10. The speaker's words were moving but irrelevant.
As used in this sentence, the word *irrelevant* means MOST NEARLY

    A. insincere
    B. not based upon facts
    C. not bearing upon the subject under discussion
    D. self-contradictory

10._

11. The breakdown of the machine was due to a defective gasket.
As used in this sentence, the word *gasket* means MOST NEARLY

    A. filter   B. piston
    C. sealer   D. transmission

11._

12. The noise of the pneumatic drill disturbed the teacher.
As used in this sentence, the word *pneumatic* means MOST NEARLY

    A. air pressure   B. electricity
    C. internal combustion   D. water pressure

12._

13. He exercised the prerogatives of his office with moderation.
As used in this sentence, the word *prerogatives* means MOST NEARLY

    A. burdens   B. duties
    C. opportunities   D. privileges

13._

14. He made his decisions after a cursory examination of the facts.
As used in this sentence, the word *cursory* means MOST NEARLY

    A. biased   B. critical
    C. exhaustive   D. hasty

14._

15. John was appointed provisional chairman of the arrange-ments committee.
As used in this sentence, the word *provisional* means MOST NEARLY

    A. official   B. permanent
    C. temporary   D. unofficial

15._

16. After the bush is planted, the ground around it should be tamped.
As used in this sentence, the word *tamped* means MOST NEARLY

    A. loosened   B. packed   C. raked   D. watered

16._

17. The volcano was dormant during the time I visited the island.
As used in this sentence, the word *dormant* means MOST NEARLY

    A. erupting   B. extinct
    C. inactive   D. threatening

17._

18. A starter's gun is not considered to be a lethal weapon.
As used in this sentence, the word *lethal* means MOST NEARLY

    A. criminal   B. deadly   C. offensive   D. reliable

18._

19. At the crucial moment, the seismograph failed to function. As used in this sentence, the word *seismograph* means MOST NEARLY an instrument for measuring

    A. earthquakes   B. heartbeats
    C. humidity   D. nuclear radiation

19._

20. The supervisor's instructions were terse.
    As used in this sentence, the word *terse* means MOST NEARLY

    20.____

    A. detailed   B. harsh   C. vague   D. concise

21. He did not wish to evade these issues.
    As used in this sentence, the word *evade* means MOST NEARLY

    21.____

    A. avoid   B. examine   C. settle   D. discuss

22. The prospects for an early settlement were dubious.
    As used in this sentence, the word *dubious* means MOST NEARLY

    22.____

    A. strengthened   B. uncertain
    C. weakened   D. cheerful

23. The visitor was morose.
    As used in this sentence, the word *morose* means MOST NEARLY

    23.____

    A. curious   B. gloomy   C. impatient   D. timid

24. He was unwilling to impede the work of his unit.
    As used in this sentence, the word *impede* means MOST NEARLY

    24.____

    A. carry out   B. criticize   C. praise   D. hinder

25. The remuneration was unsatisfactory.
    As used in this sentence, the word *remuneration* means MOST NEARLY

    25.____

    A. payment   B. summary
    C. explanation   D. estimate

26. A *recurring* problem is one that

    26.____

    A. replaces a problem that existed previously
    B. is unexpected
    C. has long been overlooked
    D. comes up from time to time

27. His subordinates were aware of this magnanimous act. As used in this sentence, the word *magnanimous* means MOST NEARLY

    27.____

    A. insolent   B. shrewd
    C. unselfish   D. threatening

28. The new employee is a zealous worker.
    As used in this sentence, the word *zealous* means MOST NEARLY

    28.____

    A. awkward   B. untrustworthy
    C. enthusiastic   D. skillful

29. To *impair* means MOST NEARLY to

    29.____

    A. weaken   B. conceal   C. improve   D. expose

30. The unit head was in a quandary.
    As used in this sentence, the word *quandary* means MOST NEARLY

    30.____

    A. violent dispute   B. puzzling predicament
    C. angry mood   D. strong position

31. His actions were judicious.
    As used in this sentence, the word *judicious* means MOST NEARLY

    A. wise   B. biased   C. final   D. limited

32. His report contained many irrelevant statements.
    As used in this sentence, the word *irrelevant* means MOST NEARLY

    A. unproven   B. not pertinent
    C. hard to understand   D. insincere

33. He was not present at the inception of the program.
    As used in this sentence, the word *inception* means MOST NEARLY

    A. beginning   B. discussion
    C. conclusion   D. rejection

34. The word *solicitude* means MOST NEARLY

    A. request   B. isolation
    C. seriousness   D. concern

35. He was asked to pacify the visitor.
    As used in this sentence, the word *pacify* means MOST NEARLY

    A. escort   B. interview   C. calm   D. detain

36. To say that a certain document is *authentic* means MOST NEARLY that it is

    A. fictitious   B. well written
    C. priceless   D. genuine

37. A clerk who is *meticulous* in performing his work is one who is

    A. alert to improved techniques
    B. likely to be erratic and unpredictable
    C. excessively careful of small details
    D. slovenly and inaccurate

38. A pamphlet which is *replete* with charts and graphs is one which

    A. deals with the construction of charts and graphs
    B. is full of charts and graphs
    C. substitutes illustrations for tabulated data
    D. is in need of charts and graphs

39. His former secretary was diligent in carrying out her duties.
    The word *diligent* means MOST NEARLY

    A. incompetent   B. cheerful
    C. careless   D. industrious

40. To *supersede* means MOST NEARLY to

    A. take the place of   B. come before
    C. be in charge of   D. divide into equal parts

31.___
32.___
33.___
34.___
35.___
36.___
37.___
38.___
39.___
40.___

41. A person is a *tyro* if he is MOST NEARLY a   41.____

    A. charlatan   B. novice
    C. scholar   D. talebearer

42. A tenant who is *adamant* in his complaints about the noise emanating from the neighbor-   42.____
    ing apartment is MOST NEARLY

    A. belligerent   B. justified
    C. petty   D. unyielding

43. The assistant, according to his supervisor's report, had performed his tasks assiduously.   43.____
    The word *assiduously* means MOST NEARLY

    A. diligently   B. expertly
    C. inefficiently   D. reluctantly

44. The current exigency of affairs at the Authority was given as the reason for the decision. 44.____
    The word *exigency* means MOST NEARLY

    A. conduct   B. investigation
    C. trend   D. urgency

45. The discovery of the defalcation was made by the manager. The word *defalcation* means   45.____
    MOST NEARLY

    A. damage   B. error   C. fraud   D. theft

46. The halcyon days that followed could not have been predicted.   46.____
    The word *halcyon* means MOST NEARLY

    A. eventful   B. festive
    C. frenzied   D. untroubled

47. The assistant submitted a sent_ious report after he had made his investigation.   47.____
    The word *sententious* means MOST NEARLY

    A. laudatory   B. pithy
    C. tentative   D. unfavorable

48. An assistant should be characterized as *saturnine* if he is MOST NEARLY   48.____

    A. apathetic   B. enigmatic   C. gloomy   D. sarcastic

49. A situation arising at a project is *anomalous* if the situation is MOST NEARLY   49.____

    A. irritating   B. perplexing
    C. recurrent   D. unusual

50. The Housing Authority did what it could to palliate the condition about which the tenants   50.____
    had complained.
    The word *palliate* means MOST NEARLY

    A. reconsider   B. rectify
    C. relieve   D. remedy

KEY (CORRECT ANSWERS)

1.	C	11.	C	21.	A	31.	A	41.	B
2.	B	12.	A	22.	B	32.	B	42.	D
3.	A	13.	D	23.	B	33.	A	43.	A
4.	C	14.	D	24.	D	34.	D	44.	D
5.	B	15.	C	25.	A	35.	C	45.	D
6.	A	16.	B	26.	D	36.	D	46.	D
7.	A	17.	C	27.	C	37.	C	47.	B
8.	B	18.	B	28.	C	38.	B	48.	C
9.	D	19.	A	29.	A	39.	D	49.	D
10.	C	20.	D	30.	B	40.	A	50.	C

———

TEST 3

DIRECTIONS: Each question or incomplete statement is followed by several suggested answers or completions. Select the one that BEST answers the question or completes the statement. *PRINT THE LETTER OF THE CORRECT ANSWER IN THE SPACE AT THE RIGHT.*

1. The employees were skeptical about the usefulness of the new procedure. The word *skeptical,* as used in this sentence, means MOST NEARLY

    A. enthusiastic
    C. doubtful
    B. indifferent
    D. misinformed

    1.____

2. He presented abstruse reasons in defense of his proposal. The word *abstruse,* as used in this sentence, means MOST NEARLY

    A. unnecessary under the circumstances
    B. apparently without merit or value
    C. hard to be understood
    D. obviously sound

    2.____

3. A program of austerity is in effect in many countries. The word *austerity,* as used in this sentence, means MOST NEARLY

    A. rigorous self-restraint
    C. rugged individualism
    B. military censorship
    D. self-indulgence

    3.____

4. The terms of the contract were abrogated at the last meeting of the board. The word *abrogated,* as used in this sentence, means MOST NEARLY

    A. discussed
    C. agreed upon
    B. summarized
    D. annulled

    4.____

5. The enforcement of stringent regulations is a difficult task. The word *stringent,* as used in this sentence, means MOST NEARLY

    A. unreasonable
    C. unpopular
    B. strict
    D. obscure

    5.____

6. You should not disparage the value of his suggestions. The word *disparage,* as used in this sentence, means MOST NEARLY

    A. ignore
    C. belittle
    B. exaggerate
    D. reveal

    6.____

7. The employee's conduct was considered reprehensible by his superior. The word *reprehensible,* as used in this sentence, means MOST NEARLY

    A. worthy of reward or honor
    B. in accordance with rules and regulations
    C. detrimental to efficiency and morale
    D. deserving of censure or rebuke

    7.____

8. He said he would emulate the persistence of his co-workers. The word *emulate,* as used in this sentence, means MOST NEARLY

    A. strive to equal
    C. encourage
    B. acknowledge
    D. attach no significance to

    8.____

9. The revised regulations on discipline contained several mitigating provisions.
   The word *mitigating,* as used in this sentence, means MOST NEARLY

      A. making more effective   B. containing contradictions
      C. rendering less harsh   D. producing much criticism

   9.__

10. The arrival of the inspector at the office on that day was fortuitous.
    The word *fortuitous,* as used in this sentence, means MOST NEARLY

       A. accidental   B. unfortunate
       C. prearranged   D. desirable

    10.__

11. The development of the program received its real impetus in the recent action of the
    commissioner.
    The word *impetus,* as used in this sentence, means MOST NEARLY

       A. formulation   B. impediment
       C. implementation   D. stimulus

    11.__

12. However, the purpose is not to be pedantic but to be practical.
    The word *pedantic,* as used in this sentence, means MOST NEARLY

       A. affected   B. philosophical
       C. progressive   D. scientific

    12.__

13. There is much just criticism of the dilatoriness with which many large organizations per-
    form their work and the red tape that is required in the discharge of official duties.
    The word *dilatoriness,* as used in this sentence, means MOST NEARLY

       A. complications   B. delay
       C. dilations   D. splendor

    13.__

14. If it appears that this report moves occasionally into the general field of administrative
    problems, your indulgence is asked, since it seems to us that voices should be heard
    wherever possible in behalf of sound, scientific public administration.
    The word *indulgence,* as used in this sentence, means MOST NEARLY

       A. criticism   B. assistance
       C. forbearance   D. concentration

    14.__

15. The supervisor's chief functions as leader are to develop the individuals under him and to
    integrate them into a cooperative team.
    The word *integrate,* as used in this sentence, means MOST NEARLY

       A. develop   B. mold   C. unify   D. work

    15.__

16. The impression is widespread that it is inherently impossible to secure the same effi-
    ciency and economy in the administration of public affairs that can be secured in the con-
    duct of private undertakings.
    The word *inherently,* as used in this sentence, means MOST NEARLY

       A. admittedly   B. internally
       C. naturally   D. practically

    16.__

17. The production manager had followed an opportunistic policy and had met new require-   17.____
ments as they appeared.
The word *opportunistic,* as used in this sentence, means MOST NEARLY

    A. efficient   B. expedient
    C. farsighted   D. important

18. Therein is epitomized the agricultural revolution which, hand in hand with the industrial   18.____
revolution, is rebuilding the country and our social life.
The word *epitomized,* as used in this sentence, means MOST NEARLY

    A. annotated   B. described
    C. expatriated   D. summarized

19. A periodic appraisal of the method of effectuating decisions is important.   19.____
The word *effectuating,* as used in this sentence, means MOST NEARLY

    A. affecting   B. developing
    C. fulfilling   D. making

20. The classifications of filing material in this office are, then, artificial and overlapping, and   20.____
are designed for transient convenience.
The word *transient,* as used in this sentence, means MOST NEARLY

    A. basic   B. local   C. operating   D. temporary

21. From a research standpoint, there is hardly a paucity of material for us to consider.   21.____
The word *paucity*, as used in this sentence, means MOST NEARLY

    A. abundance   B. adequate amount
    C. insufficiency   D. unsatisfactory quality

22. This assignment was handled expeditiously.   22.____
The word *expeditiously* means MOST NEARLY

    A. clumsily   B. without preparation
    C. speedily   D. on a trial basis

23. Miss Lind is scrupulous in performing her duties.   23.____
The word *scrupulous* means MOST NEARLY

    A. slow   B. conscientious
    C. careless   D. gracious

24. To *apprise* means MOST NEARLY to   24.____

    A. award   B. inform
    C. dispossess   D. discover

25. His report on this matter is opportune.   25.____
The word *opportune* means MOST NEARLY

    A. timely   B. biased   C. hostile   D. hopeful

26. His actions had a deleterious effect on the other employees.
The word *deleterious* means MOST NEARLY

    A. restraining
    C. harmful
    B. highly pleasing
    D. misleading

27. The size of the staff was increased, and the gain in output was commensurate.
The word *commensurate* means MOST NEARLY

    A. praiseworthy
    C. of equal extent
    B. enormous
    D. trivial in proportion

28. Miss Hunter is assiduous in keeping these records.
The word *assiduous* means MOST NEARLY

    A. negligent
    C. unrestricted
    B. untrained
    D. diligent

29. His bookkeeper said that our account was dormant.
The word *dormant* means MOST NEARLY

    A. inadequate
    C. inactive
    B. transferred
    D. overdrawn

30. The supervisor's criticisms were caustic.
The word *caustic* means MOST NEARLY

    A. sarcastic and severe
    C. ominous but justified
    B. unfair and undeserved
    D. fitful and unsteady

31. The word *impediment* means MOST NEARLY

    A. hindrance
    C. insinuation
    B. trick or deception
    D. urgent matter

32. This procedure did not preclude errors in judgment.
The word *preclude* means MOST NEARLY

    A. arise from
    C. account for
    B. prevent
    D. define

33. The statements made at the initial conference were retracted at a subsequent meeting.
The word *retracted* means MOST NEARLY

    A. developed
    C. endorsed
    B. criticized
    D. withdrawn

34. He was unwilling to supplant his immediate superior.
The word *supplant* means MOST NEARLY

    A. fill the needs of
    C. take the place of
    B. request aid from
    D. withhold support for

35. Miss Olin has a prepossessing manner.
The word *prepossessing* means MOST NEARLY

    A. authoritative
    C. apologetic
    B. likable
    D. deceiving

36. The methods used to solve these critical problems were analogous.
The word *analogous* means MOST NEARLY

    A. similar
    C. clever
    B. unconventional
    D. unsound

36.____

37. This letter appears to have been written by some indigent person.
The word *indigent,* as used in this sentence, means MOST NEARLY

    A. foreign-born
    C. uneducated
    B. needy
    D. angry

37.____

38. The conference began under auspicious circumstances.
The word *auspicious,* as used in this sentence, means MOST NEARLY

    A. favorable
    C. questionable
    B. chaotic
    D. threatening

38.____

39. An inordinate amount of work was assigned to the newly appointed clerk.
The word *inordinate,* as used in this sentence, means MOST NEARLY

    A. unanticipated
    C. inexcusable
    B. adequate
    D. excessive

39.____

40. The report which was obtained surreptitiously was very detailed and fully documented.
The word *surreptitiously,* as used in this sentence, means MOST NEARLY

    A. stealthily
    C. with great difficulty
    B. a short time ago
    D. unexpectedly

40.____

41. We all knew him to be a man of probity.
The word *probity,* as used in this sentence, means MOST NEARLY

    A. culture
    C. integrity
    B. proven ability
    D. dignity and poise

41.____

42. He made a cursory study of the problem before starting on the assignment.
The word *cursory,* as used in this sentence, means MOST NEARLY

    A. detailed   B. secret   C. hasty   D. methodical

42.____

43. The regulation had a salutary effect upon the members of the staff.
The word *salutary,* as used in this sentence, means MOST NEARLY

    A. disturbing
    C. confusing
    B. beneficial
    D. premature

43.____

44. The solicitous supervisor discussed the employee's grievances with them.
The word *solicitous,* as used in this sentence, means MOST NEARLY

    A. concerned
    C. wise
    B. impartial
    D. experienced

44.____

45. The employee categorically denied all responsibility for the error.
The word *categorically,* as used in this sentence, means MOST NEARLY

    A. repeatedly
    C. hesitantly
    B. loudly
    D. absolutely

45.____

46. No stipend was specified in the agreement.
The word *stipend,* as used in this sentence, means MOST NEARLY

   A. statement of working conditions
   B. receipt for payment
   C. compensation for services
   D. delivery date

46.___

47. The supervisor pointed out that the focus of the study was not clear.
The word *focus,* as used in this sentence, means MOST NEARLY

   A. end   B. objective   C. follow-up   D. location

47.___

48. The faculty of the department agreed that the departmental program was deficient.
The word *deficient,* as used in this sentence, means MOST NEARLY

   A. excellent   B. inadequate
   C. demanding   D. sufficient

48.___

49. The secretary was asked to type a rough draft of a college course syllabus.
The word *syllabus,* as used in this sentence, means MOST NEARLY

   A. directory of departments and services
   B. examination schedule
   C. outline of a course of study
   D. rules and regulations

49.___

50. The college offered a variety of seminars to upperclassmen.
The word *seminars,* as used in this sentence, means MOST NEARLY

   A. reading courses with no formal supervision
   B. study courses for small groups of students engaged in research under a teacher
   C. guidance conferences with grade advisors
   D. work experiences in different occupational fields

50.___

KEY (CORRECT ANSWERS)

1. C	11. D	21. C	31. A	41. C
2. C	12. A	22. C	32. B	42. C
3. A	13. B	23. B	33. D	43. B
4. D	14. C	24. B	34. C	44. A
5. B	15. C	25. A	35. B	45. D
6. C	16. C	26. C	36. A	46. C
7. D	17. B	27. C	37. B	47. B
8. A	18. D	28. D	38. A	48. B
9. C	19. C	29. C	39. D	49. C
10. A	20. D	30. A	40. A	50. B

PREPARING WRITTEN MATERIAL

I. COMMENTARY

The need to communicate — clearly, swiftly, completely, effectively — is basic to all organizations, agencies, departments — public and private, large and small.

Communication is accomplished by employing one or more of the accepted forms of communication, singly and/or together — oral (verbal), written, visual, electronic, etc.

The method most often used to reach large numbers or groups of persons to achieve and ensure clarity, correctness, comprehension, uniformity, and permanence of effect, is through the preparation and issuance of written materials, e.g., notices, statements, letters, reports, descriptions, explanations, expositions, schedules, summaries, etc.

Preparing written material clearly and correctly is, therefore, a dutiable function of every regular and senior employee, foreman, supervisor, manager, administrator, director, and this question-type is often used as a basic, integral part of various selection processes.

Questions involving correctness of expression usually appear on career written examinations as well as on other types of general tests.

While this question-type may take several forms, the two most usual presentations are the single-sentence type, which is to be evaluated as correct or incorrect on one of several bases, and the multiple-sentence type, involving four or five sentences, one of which is to be denoted as correct (or incorrect) for reasons of grammar and usage, or correctness of expression.

DIRECTIONS AND SAMPLE QUESTIONS

DIRECTIONS

Each of the sentences numbered I and II may be classified under one of the following four categories:
  A. *Faulty* because of incorrect grammar or word usage
  B. *Faulty* because of incorrect punctuation
  C. *Faulty* because of incorrect capitalization or incorrect spelling
  D. *Correct*

Examine each sentence carefully to determine under which of the above four options it is best classified. Then, in the space to the right, print the capital letter preceding the option which is the best of the four suggested above.

SAMPLE QUESTIONS

I. One of our clerks were promoted yesterday.   I. ___

   The subject of this sentence is "one," so the verb should be "was promoted" instead of "were promoted." Since the sentence is incorrect because of bad grammar, the answer to Sample Question I is (A).

II. Between you and me, I would prefer not going there.   II. ___

   Since this sentence is correct, the answer to Sample Question II is (D).

PREPARING WRITTEN MATERIAL

II. COMMON ERRORS/CORRECT USES

Common Errors in Usage	Correct Usage
1. being that for since	1. Since he was late, he was not admitted.
2. like for as	2. She smiles as her father does.
3. off of for off	3. He took his hat off his head.
4. different than for different from	4. Your pen is different from mine.
5. quick for quickly	5. Go quickly!
6. careful for carefully	6. He laid the tray down carefully.
7. sure for surely	7. The boy was surely happy to hear this.
8. good for well	8. I cannot hear well.
9. nothing for anything.	9. I didn't see anything.
10. most for almost	10. Almost everyone was there.
11. real for really	11. The baby is really beautiful.
12. this here for this	12. This ball is broken.
13. swell for excellent	13. That was an excellent play.
14. well for good	14. She looks good in her new suit.
15. those for that (kind)	15. I prefer that kind of cigarettes.
16. less for fewer	16. We have fewer bad marks than they.
17. them for those	17. Please take those knives away.
18. they for he	18. People can be what they want to be.
19. him for he (after than)	19. I am younger than he.
20. their for his	20. Every soldier will do his duty.
21. who for whom	21. Whom do you think I met today?
22. whom for who	22. Who do you think it was?
23. I for me	23. Between you and me ...
24. are for is	24. Everybody is here.
25. tore for torn	25. He had torn the manuscript in two.
26. wrote for written	26. I have written a play.
27. busted for burst	27. The bubble burst.
28. seen for saw	28. I saw the new boy.
29. done for did	29. He did it.
30. graduated for graduated from	30. He graduated from Lincoln High.
31. irregardless for regardless	31. Regardless of the weather, we will fly.
32. am living for have been living	32. I have been living here for a month.
33. laying for lying	33. He was lying on the ground.
34. leave for let	34. Let him go.
35. should of for should have	35. I should have thought of that.
36. except for accept	36. I accept your apology.
37. besides for beside	37. I shall sit beside you.
38. affect for effect	38. The motion picture HOLOCAUST had a great effect on all who saw it.
39. amount for number	39. We have a large number of books in the library.
40. kind of a for kind of	40. What kind of car do you have?

EXAMINATION SECTION
Preparing Written Material

Directions: Each short paragraph below is followed by four restatements or summaries of the information contained within it. Select the one that most completely and accurately restates the information or opinion given in the paragraph. *PRINT THE LETTER OF THE CORRECT ANSWER IN THE SPACE AT THE RIGHT.*

1)   India's night jasmine, or hurshinghar, is different from most flowering plants, in that its flowers are closed during the day, and open after dark. The scientific reason for this is probably that the plant has avoided competing with other flowers for pollinating insects and birds, and relies instead on the service of nocturnal bats that are drawn to the flower's nectar. According to an old Indian legend, however, the flowers sprouted from the funeral ashes of a beautiful young girl who had fallen hopelessly in love with the sun.

1. _____

A.   Despite the Indian legend that explains why the hurshinghar's flowers open at dusk, scientists believe it has to do with competition for available pollinators.
B.   The Indian hurshinghar's closure of its flowers during the day is due to a lack of available pollinators.
C.   The hurshinghar of India has evolved an unhealthy dependency on nocturnal bats.
D.   Like most myths, the Indian legend of the hurshinghar's night-flowering has been disproved by science.

2)   Charles Lindbergh's trans-Atlantic flight from New York to Paris made him an international hero in 1927, but he lived nearly another fifty years, and by most accounts they weren't terribly happy ones. The two greatest tragedies of his life—the 1932 kidnapping and murder of his oldest son, and an unshakeable reputation as a Nazi sympathizer during World War II—he blamed squarely on the rabid media hounds who stalked his every move.

2. _____

A.   Despite the fact that Charles Lindbergh had a hand in the two greatest tragedies of his life, he insisted on blaming the media for his problems.
B.   Charles Lindbergh lived a largely unhappy life after the glory of his 1927 trans-Atlantic flight, and he blamed his unhappiness on media attention.
C.   Charles Lindbergh's later life was marked by despair and disillusionment.
D.   Because of the rabid media attention sparked by Charles Lindbergh's 1927 trans-Atlantic flight, he would later consider it the last happy event of his life.

3)   The United States, one of the world's youngest nations in the early nineteenth century, had yet to spread its wings in terms of foreign affairs, preferring to remain isolated and opposed to meddling in the affairs of others. But the fact remained that as a young nation situated on the opposite side of the globe from Europe, Africa, and Asia, the United States had much work to do in establishing relations with the rest of the world. So, too, as the European colonial powers continued to battle for influence in North and South America, did the United States come to believe that it was proper for them to keep these nations from encroaching into their sphere of influence.

3. _____

A.   The roots of the Monroe Doctrine can be traced to the foreign policy shift of the United States during the early nineteenth century.

B.   In the early nineteenth century, the United States shifted its foreign policy to reflect a growing desire to actively protect its interests in the Western Hemisphere.

C.   In the early nineteenth century, the United States was too young and undeveloped to have devised much in the way of foreign policy.

D.   The United States adopted a more aggressive foreign policy in the early nineteenth century in order to become a diplomatic player on the world stage.

4)   Hertha Ayrton, a nineteenth-century Englishwoman, pursued a career in science during a time when most women were not given the opportunity to go to college. Her series of successes led to her induction into the Institution of Electrical Engineers in 1899, when she was the first woman to receive this professional honor. Her most noted accomplishment was the research and invention of an anti-gas fan that the British War Office used in the trench warfare of World War I.

4. _____

A.   The British Army's success in World War I can be partly attributed to Hertha Ayrton, a groundbreaking British scientist.

B.   Hertha Ayrton was the first woman to be inducted into the Institution of Electrical Engineers.

C.   The injustices of nineteenth-century England were no match for the brilliant mind of Hertha Ayrton.

D.   Hertha Ayrton defied the restrictions of her society by building a successful scientific career.

5)   Scientists studying hyenas in Tanzania's Ngorongoro Crater have   5. _____
observed that hyena clans have evolved a system of territoriality that allows
each clan a certain space to hunt within the 100-square-mile area. These
territories are not marked by natural boundaries, but by droppings and excre-
tions from the hyenas' scent glands. Usually, the hyenas take these boundary
lines very seriously; some hyena clans have been observed abandoning their
pursuit of certain prey after the prey has crossed into another territory, even
though no members of the neighboring clan are anywhere in sight.

A.   The hyenas of Ngorongoro Crater illustrate that the best way to peace-
fully coexist within a limited territory is to strictly delineate and defend
territorial borders.
B.   While most territorial boundaries are marked using geographical
features, the hyenas of Ngorongoro Crater have devised another method.
C.   The hyena clans of Ngorongoro Crater, in order to co-exist within a
limited hunting territory, have developed a method of marking strict territorial
boundaries.
D.   As with most species, the hyenas of Ngorongoro Crater have proven
the age-old motto: "To the victor go the spoils."

6)   The flood control policy of the U.S. Army Corps of Engineers has long   6. _____
been an obvious feature of the American landscape—the Corps seeks to
contain the nation's rivers with an enormous network of dams and levees,
"channelizing" rivers into small, confined routes that will stay clear of settled
floodplains when rivers rise. As a command of the U.S. Army, the Corps
seems to have long seen the nation's rivers as an enemy to be fought; one of
the agency's early training films speaks of the Corps' "battle" with its adversary, Mother Nature.

A.   The dams and levees built by the U.S. Army Corps of Engineers have
at least defeated their adversary, Mother Nature.
B.   The flood control policy of the U.S. Army Corps of Engineers has
often reflected a military point of view, making the nation's rivers into en-
emies that must be defeated.
C.   When one realizes that the flood policy of the U.S. Army Corps of
Engineers has always relied on a kind of military strategy, it is only possible
to view the Corps' efforts as a failure.
D.   By damming and channelizing the nation's rivers, the U.S. Army
Corps of Engineers have made America's floodplains safe for farming and
development.

7)   Frogs with extra legs or missing legs have been showing up with   7. _____
greater frequency over the past decade, and scientists have been baffled by the
cause. Some researchers have concluded that pesticide runoff from farms is to
blame; others say a common parasite, the trematode, is the culprit. Now, a
new study suggests that both these factors in combination have disturbed
normal development in many frogs, leading to the abnormalities.

A.   Despite several studies, scientists still have no idea what is causing the
widespread incidence of deformities among aquatic frogs.
B.   In the debate over what is causing the increase in frog deformities,
environmentalists tend to blame pesticide runoff, while others blame a common parasite, the trematode.
C.   A recent study suggests that both pesticide runoff and natural parasites
have contributed to the increasing rate of deformities in frogs.
D.   Because of their aquatic habitat, frogs are among the most susceptible
organisms to chemical and environmental change, and this is illustrated by the
increasing rate of physical deformities among frog populations.

8)   The builders of the Egyptian pyramids, to insure that each massive   8. _____
structure was built on a completely flat surface, began by cutting a network of
criss-crossing channels into the pyramid's mapped-out ground space and
partly filling the channels with water. Because the channels were all interconnected, the water was distributed evenly throughout the channel system, and
all the workers had to do to level their building surface was cut away any rock
above the waterline.

A.   The modern carpenter's level uses a principle that was actually invented several centuries ago by the builders of the Egyptian pyramids.
B.   The discovery of the ancient Egyptians' sophisticated construction
techniques is a quiet argument against the idea that they were built by slaves.
C.   The use of water to insure that the pyramids were level mark the
Egyptians as one of the most scientifically advanced of the ancient civilizations.
D.   The builders of the Egyptian pyramids used a simple but ingenious
method for ensuring a level building surface with interconnected channels of
water.

9)   Thunderhead Mountain, a six-hundred-foot-high formation of granite   9. _____
in the Black Hills of South Dakota, is slowly undergoing a transformation that
will not be finished for more than a century, when what remains of the mountain will have become the largest sculpture in the world. The statue, begun in
1947 by a Boston sculptor named Henry Ziolkowski, is still being carved and
blasted by his wife and children into the likeness of Crazy Horse, the legendary chief of the Sioux tribe of American natives. The enormity of the sculpture—the planned length of one of the figure's arms is 263 feet—is understandable, given the historical greatness of Crazy Horse.

A.   Only a hero as great as Crazy Horse could warrant a sculpture so large
that it will take more than a century to complete.
B.   In 1947, sculptor Henry Ziolkowski began work on what he imagined
would be the largest sculpture in the world—even though he knew he would
not live to see it completed.
C.   The huge Black Hills sculpture of the great Sioux chief Crazy Horse,
still being carried out by the family of Henry Ziolkowski, will some day be
the largest sculpture in the world.
D.   South Dakota's Thunderhead Mountain will soon be the site of the
world's largest sculpture, a statue of the Sioux chief Crazy Horse.

10)   Because they were some of the first explorers to venture into the   10. _____
western frontier of North America, the French were responsible for the nam-
ing of several native tribes. Some of these names were poorly conceived—the
worst of which was perhaps Eskimo, the name for the natives of the far North,
which translates roughly as "eaters of raw flesh." The name is incorrect; these
people have always cooked their fish and game, and they now call themselves
the Inuit, a native term that means "the people."

A.   The first to explore much of North America's western frontier were the
French, and they usually gave improper or poorly-informed names to the
native tribes.
B.   The Eskimos of North America have never eaten raw flesh, so it is
curious that the French would give them a name that means "eaters of raw
flesh."
C.   The Inuit have fought for many years to overcome the impression that
they eat raw flesh.
D.   Like many native tribes, the Inuit were once incorrectly named by
French explorers, but they have since corrected the mistake themselves.

11)   Of the 30,000 species of spiders worldwide, only a handful are danger-   11. _____
ous to human beings, but this doesn't prevent many people from having a
powerful fear of all spiders, whether they are venomous or not. The leading
scientific theory about arachnophobia, as this fear is known, is that far in our
evolutionary past, some species of spider must have presented a serious
enough threat to people that the sight of a star-shaped body or an eight-legged
walk was coded into our genes as a danger signal.

A.   Scientists theorize that peoples' widespread fear of spiders can be
traced to an ancient spider species that was dangerous enough to trigger this
fearful reaction.
B.   The fear known as arachnophobia is triggered by the sight of a star-
shaped body or an eight-legged walk.
C.   Because most spiders have a uniquely shaped body that triggers a
human fear response, many humans are afflicted with the fear of spiders
known as arachnophobia.
D.   Though only a few of the planet's 30,000 spider species are dangerous
to people, many people have an unreasonable fear of them.

12)   From the 1970s to the 1990s, the percentage of Americans living in the   12. _____
suburbs climbed from 37% to 47%. In the latter part of the 1990s, a movement emerged that questioned the good of such a population shift—or at least,
the good of the speed and manner in which this suburban land was being
developed. Often, people began to argue, the planning of such growth was
flawed, resulting in a phenomenon that has become known as suburban
"sprawl," or the growth of suburban orbits around cities at rates faster than
infrastructures could support, and in ways that are damaging to the environment.

A.   The term "urban sprawl" was coined in the 1990s, when the movement
against unchecked suburban development began to gather momentum.
B.   In the 1980s and 1990s, home builders benefited from a boom in their
most favored demographic segment—suburban new-home buyers.
C.   Suburban development tends to suffer from poor planning, which can
lead to a lower quality of life for residents.
D.   The surge in suburban residences in the late twentieth century was
criticized by many as "sprawl" that could not be supported by existing resources.

13)   Medicare, a $200 billion-a-year program, processes 1 billion claims   13. _____
annually, and in the year 2000, the computer system that handles these claims
came under criticism. The General Accounting Office branded Medicare's
financial management system as outdated and inadequate—one in a series of
studies and reports warning that the program is plagued with duplication,
overcharges, double billings and confusion among users.

A.   The General Accounting Office's 2000 report proves that Medicare is a
bloated bureaucracy in need of substantial reform.
B.   Medicare's confusing computer network is an example of how the
federal government often neglects the programs that mean the most to average
American citizens.
C.   In the year 2000, the General Accounting Office criticized Medicare's
financial accounting network as inefficient and outdated.
D.   Because it has to handle so many claims each year, Medicare's financial accounting system often produces redundancies and errors.

14)   The earliest known writing materials were thin clay tablets, used in   14. _____
Mesopotamia more than 5,000 years ago. Although the tablets were cheap
and easy to produce, they had two major disadvantages: they were difficult to
store, and once the clay had dried and hardened a person could not write on
them. The ancient Egyptians later discovered a better writing material—the
thin bark of the papyrus reed, a plant that grew near the mouth of the Nile
River, which could be peeled into long strips, woven into a mat-like layer,
pounded flat with heavy mallets, and then dried in the sun.

A.   The Egyptians, after centuries of frustration with clay writing tablets,
were finally forced to invent a better writing surface.
B.   With the bark of the papyrus reed, ancient Egyptians made a writing
material that overcame the disadvantages of clay tablets.
C.   The Egyptian invention of the papyrus scroll was necessitated in part
by a relative lack of available clay.
D.   The word "paper" can be traced to the innovations of the Egyptians,
who made the first paper-like writing material from the bark of papyrus plant.

15)   In 1850, the German pianomaker Heinrich Steinweg and his family   15. _____
stepped off an immigrant ship in New York City, threw themselves into competition with dozens of other established craftsmen, and defeated them all by
reinventing the instrument. The company they created commanded the market
for nearly the next century and a half, while their competitors—some of the
most acclaimed pianomakers in the business—faded into obscurity. And all
the while, Steinway & Sons, through their sponsorship and encouragement of
the world's most distinguished pianists, helped define the cultural life of the
young United States.

A.   The Steinways capitalized on weak competition during the mid-
nineteenth century to capture the American piano market.
B.   Because of their technical and cultural innovations, the Steinways had
an advantage over other American pianomakers.
C.   Heinrich Steinweg founded the Steinway piano empire in 1850.
D.   From humble immigrant origins, the Steinway family rose to dominate
both the pianomaking industry and American musical culture.

16)   Feng Shui, the ancient Chinese science of studying the natural   16. _____
environment's effect on a person's well-being, has gained new popularity in
the design and decoration of buildings.
Although a complex area of study, a basic premise of Feng Shui is that each
building creates a unique field of energy which affects the inhabitants of that
building or home.
In recent years, decorators and realtors have begun to offer services which
include a diagnosis of a building's Feng Shui, or energy.

A.   Feng Shui, the Chinese science of balancing environmental energies,
has been given more aesthetic quality by recent practitioners.
B.   Generally, practitioners of Feng Shui work to create balance within a
room, carefully arranging sharp and soft surfaces to create a positive environment that suits the room's primary purpose.
C.   The idea behind the Chinese "science" of Feng Shui—that objects give
off certain energies that affect a building's inhabitants—has been a difficult
one for most Westerners to accept, but it is gaining in popularity.
D.   The ancient Chinese science of Feng Shui, which studies the balance
of energies in a person's environment, has become popular among those who
design and decorate buildings.

17) Because the harsh seasonal variations of the Kansas plains make survival difficult for most plant life, the area is dominated by tall, sturdy grasses. The only tree that has been able to survive—and prosper—throughout the wide expanse of prairie is the cottonwood, which can take root and grow in the most extreme climatic conditions. Sometimes a storm will shear off a living branch and carry it downstream, where it may snag along a sandbar and take root.

17. _____

A.   Among the plant life of the Kansas plains, the only tree is the cottonwood.
B.   The only prosperous tree on the Kansas plains is the cottonwood, which can take root and grow in a wide range of conditions.
C.   Only the cottonwood, whose branches can grow after being broken off and washed down a river, is capable of surviving the climatic extremes of the Kansas plains.
D.   Because it is the most widespread and hardiest tree on the Kansas plains, the cottonwood had become a symbol of pioneer grit and fortitude.

18) In the twenty-first century, it's easy to see the automobile as the keystone of American popular culture. Subtract linen dusters, driving goggles, and women's *crepe de chine* veils from our history, and you've taken the Roaring out of the Twenties. Take away the ducktail haircuts, pegged pants and upturned collars from the teen Car Cult of the Fifties, and the decade isn't nearly as Fabulous. Were the chromed and tailfinned muscle cars of the automobile's Golden Age modeled after us, or were we mimicking them?

18. _____

A.   Ever since its invention, the automobile has shaped American culture.
B.   Many of the familiar names we give historical eras, such as "Roaring Twenties" and "Fabulous Fifties," were given because of the predominance of the automobile.
C.   Americans' tastes in clothing have been determined primarily by the cars they drive.
D.   Teenagers have had a fascination for automobiles ever since the motorcar was first invented.

19) Since the 1960s, an important issue for Canada has been the status of minority French-speaking Canadians, especially in the province of Quebec, whose inhabitants make up 30% of the Canadian population and trace their ancestry back to a Canada that preceded British influence. In response to pressure from Quebec nationalists, the government in 1982 added a Charter of Rights to the constitution, restoring important rights that dated back to the time of aboriginal treaties. Separatism is still a prominent issue, though successive referendums and constitutional inquiries have not resulted in any realistic progress toward Quebec's independence.

19. _____

A.   Despite the fact that Quebec's inhabitants have their roots in Canada's original settlers, they have been constantly oppressed by the descendants of those who came later, the British.

B.   It seems unavoidable that Quebec's linguistic and cultural differences with the rest of Canada will some day lead to its secession.

C.   French-speaking Quebec's activism over the last several decades has led to concessions by the Canadian government, but it seems that Quebec will remain a part of the country for some time.

D.   The inhabitants of Quebec are an aboriginal culture that has been exploited by the Canadian government for years, but they are gradually winning back their rights.

20) For years, musicians and scientists have tried to discover what it is about an eighteenth-century Stradivarius violin—which may sell for more than $1 million on today's market—that gives it its unique sound. In 1977, American scientist Joseph Nagyvary discovered that the Stradivarius is made of a spruce wood that came from Venice, where timber was stored beneath the sea, and unlike the dry-seasoned wood from which other violins were made, this spruce contains microscopic holes which add resonance to the violin's sound. Nagyvary also found the varnish used on the Stradivarius to be equally unique, containing tiny mineral crystals that appear to have come from ground-up gemstones, which would filter out high-pitched tones and give the violin a smoother sound.

20. _____

A.   After carefully studying Stradivarius violins to discover the source of their unique sound, an American scientist discovered two qualities in the construction of them that set them apart from other instruments: the wood from which they were made, and the varnish used to coat the wood.

B.   The two qualities that give the Stradivarius violin such a unique sound are the wood, which adds resonance, and the finish, which filters out high-pitched tones.

C.   The Stradivarius violin, because of the unique wood and finish used in its construction, is widely regarded as the finest string instrument ever manu-factured in the world.

D.   A close study of the Stradivarius violin has revealed that the best wood for making violins is Venetian spruce, stored underwater.

21) People who watch the display of fireflies on a clear summer evening   21. _____
are actually witnessing a complex chemical reaction called "bioluminescence," which turns certain organisms into living light bulbs. Organisms that
produce this light undergo a reaction in which oxygen combines with a chemical called lucerfin and an enzyme called luciferase. Depending on the organ-
ism, the light produced from this reaction can range from the light green of the
firefly to the bright red spots of a railroad worm.

A.   Although the function of most displays of bioluminescence is to attract
mates, as is the case with fireflies, other species rely on bioluminescence for
different purposes.
B.   Bioluminescence, a phenomenon produced by several organisms, is
the result of a chemical reaction that takes place within the body of the organ-
ism.
C.   Of all the organisms in the world, only insects are capable of display-
ing bioluminescence.
D.   Despite the fact that some organisms display bioluminescence, these
reactions produce almost no heat, which is why the light they create is sometimes referred to as cold light.

22)   The first of America's "log cabin" presidents, Andrew Jackson rose   22. _____
from humble backcountry origins to become a U.S. congressman and senator,
a renowned military hero, and the seventh president of the United States.
Among many Americans, especially those of the western frontier, he was
acclaimed as a symbol of the "new" American: self-made, strong through
closeness to nature, and endowed with a powerful moral courage.

A.   Andrew Jackson was the first American president to rise from modest
origins.
B.   Because he was born poor, President Andrew Jackson was more
popular among Americans of the western frontier.
C.   Andrew Jackson's humble background, along with his outstanding
achievements, made him into a symbol of American strength and self-suffi-
ciency.
D.   Andrew Jackson achieved success as a legislator, soldier, and president
because he was born humbly and had to work for every honor he ever received.

23)   In the past few decades, while much of the world's imagination has   23. _____
focused on the possibilities of outer space, some scientists have been exploring a different frontier—the ocean floor. Although ships have been sailing the
oceans for centuries, only recently have scientists developed vehicles strong
enough to sustain the pressure of deep-sea exploration and observation. These
fiberglass vehicles, called submersibles, are usually just big enough to take
two or three people to the deepest parts of the oceans' floors.

A.   Modern submersible vehicles, thanks to recent technological innovations, are now explore underwater cliffs, crevices and mountain ranges that
were once unreachable.
B.   While most people tend to fantasize about exploring outer space, they
should be turning toward a more accessible realm—the depths of the earth's
oceans.
C.   Because of the necessarily small size of submersible vehicles, exploration of the deep ocean is not a widespread activity.
D.   Recent technological developments have helped scientists to turn their
attention from deep space to the deep ocean.

24)   The panda—a native of the remote mountainous regions of China—   24. _____
subsists almost entirely on the tender shoots of the bamboo plant. This restric-
tive diet has allowed the panda to evolve an anatomical structure that is
completely different from that of other bears, whose paws are aligned for
running, stabbing, and scratching. The panda's paw has an over-developed
wrist bone that juts out below the other claws like a thumb, and the panda uses
this "thumb" to grip bamboo shoots while it strips them of their leaves.

A.   The panda is the only bear-like animal that feeds on vegetation, and it
has a kind of thumb to help it grip bamboo shoots.
B.   The panda's limited diet of bamboo has led it to evolve a thumb-like
appendage for grasping bamboo shoots.
C.   The panda's thumb-like appendage is a factor that limits its diet to the
shoots of the bamboo plant.
D.   Because bamboo shoots must be held tightly while eaten, the panda's
thumb-like appendage ensure that it is the only bear-like animal that eats
bamboo.

25)   The stability and security of the Balkan region remains a primary
concern for Greece in post-Cold War Europe, and Greece's active participation in peacekeeping and humanitarian operations in Georgia, Albania, and
Bosnia are substantial examples of this commitment. Due to its geopolitical
position, Greece believes it necessary to maintain, at least for now, a more
nationalized defense force than other European nations. It is Greece's hope
that the new spirit of integration and cooperation will help establish a common
European foreign affairs and defense policy that might ease some of these
regional tensions, and allow a greater level of Greek participation in NATO's
integrated military structure.

25. _____

A.   Greece's proximity to the unstable Balkan region has led it to keep a
more nationalized military, though it hopes to become more involved in a
common European defense force.
B.   The Balkan states present a greater threat to Greece than any other
European nation, and Greece has adopted a highly nationalist military force as
a result.
C.   Greece, the only Balkan state to belong to NATO, has an isolationist
approach to defense, but hopes to achieve greater integration in the
organization's combined forces.
D.   Greece's failure to become more militarily integrated with the rest of
Europe can be attributed to the failure to establish a common European de-
fense policy.

KEY (CORRECT ANSWERS)

1. A
2. B
3. B
4. D
5. C

6. B
7. C
8. D
9. C
10. D

11. A
12. D
13. C
14. B
15. D

16. D
17. B
18. A
19. C
20. A

21. B
22. C
23. D
24. B
25. A

PREPARING WRITTEN MATERIAL

PARAGRAPH REARRANGEMENT
COMMENTARY

The sentences which follow are in scrambled order. You are to rearrange them in proper order and indicate the letter choice containing the correct answer at the space at the right.

Each group of sentences in this section is actually a paragraph presented in scrambled order. Each sentence in the group has a place in that paragraph; no sentence is to be left out. You are to read each group of sentences and decide upon the best order in which to put the sentences so as to form as well-organized paragraph.

The questions in this section measure the ability to solve a problem when all the facts relevant to its solution are not given.

More specifically, certain positions of responsibility and authority require the employee to discover connections between events sometimes, apparently, unrelated. In order to do this, the employee will find it necessary to correctly infer that unspecified events have probably occurred or are likely to occur. This ability becomes especially important when action must be taken on incomplete information.

Accordingly, these questions require competitors to choose among several suggested alternatives, each of which presents a different sequential arrangement of the events. Competitors must choose the MOST logical of the suggested sequences.

In order to do so, they may be required to draw on general knowledge to infer missing concepts or events that are essential to sequencing the given events. Competitors should be careful to infer only what is essential to the sequence. The plausibility of the wrong alternatives will always require the inclusion of unlikely events or of additional chains of events which are NOT essential to sequencing the given events.

It's very important to remember that you are looking for the best of the four possible choices, and that the best choice of all may not even be one of the answers you're given to choose from.

There is no one right way to these problems. Many people have found it helpful to first write out the order of the sentences, as they would have arranged them, on their scrap paper before looking at the possible answers. If their optimum answer is there, this can save them some time. If it isn't, this method can still give insight into solving the problem. Others find it most helpful to just go through each of the possible choices, contrasting each as they go along. You should use whatever method feels comfortable, and works, for you.

While most of these types of questions are not that difficult, we've added a higher percentage of the difficult type, just to give you more practice. Usually there are only one or two questions on this section that contain such subtle distinctions that you're unable to answer confidently, and you then may find yourself stuck deciding between two possible choices, neither of which you're sure about.

———

PREPARING WRITTEN MATERIAL

EXAMINATION SECTION

DIRECTIONS: The following groups of sentences need to be arranged so that the entire passage is correctly organized from start to finish. Select the letter preceding the sequence that represents the best sentence order. *PRINT THE LETTER OF THE CORRECT ANSWER IN THE SPACE AT THE RIGHT.*

Question 1

1._____

1. The ostrich egg shell's legendary toughness makes it an excellent substitute for certain types of dishes or dinnerware, and in parts of Africa ostrich shells are cut and decorated for use as containers for water.

2. Since prehistoric times, people have used the enormous egg of the ostrich as a part of their diet, a practice which has required much patience and hard work – to hard-boil an ostrich egg takes about four hours.

3. Opening the egg's shell, which is rock hard and nearly an inch thick, requires heavy tools, such as a saw or chisel; from inside, a baby ostrich must use a hornlike projection on its beak as a miniature pick-axe to escape from the egg.

4. The offspring of all higher-order animals originate from single egg cells that are carried by mothers, and most of these eggs are relatively small, often microscopic.

5. The egg of the African ostrich, however, weighs a massive thirty pounds, making it the largest single cell on earth, and a common object of human curiosity and wonder.

The best order is
A. 5 4 1 2 3
B. 1 4 5 3 2
C. 4 2 3 5 1
D. 4 5 2 3 1

Question 2

1. Typically only a few feet high on the open sea, individual tsunami have been known to circle the entire globe two or three times if their progress is not interrupted, but are not usually dangerous until they approach the shallow water that surrounds land masses.

2. Some of the most terrifying and damaging hazards caused by earthquakes are tsunami, which were once called "tidal waves" – a poorly chosen name, since these waves have nothing to do with tides.

3. Then a wave, slowed by the sudden drag on the lower part of its moving water column, will pile upon itself, sometimes reaching a height of over 100 feet.

4. Tsunami (Japanese for "great harbor wave") are seismic waves that are caused by earthquakes near oceanic trenches, and once triggered, can travel up to 600 miles an hour on the open ocean.

5. A land-shoaling tsunami is capable of extraordinary destruction; some tsunami have deposited large boats miles inland, washed out two-foot-thick seawalls, and scattered locomotive trains over long distances.

The best order is
   A. 4 1 3 2 5
   B. 1 3 4 2 5
   C. 5 1 3 2 4
   D. 2 4 1 3 5

Question 3

1. Soon, by the 1940's, jazz was the most popular type of music among American intellectuals and college students.

2. In the early days of jazz, it was considered "lowdown" music, or music that was played only in rough, disreputable bars and taverns.

3. However, jazz didn't take long to develop from early ragtime melodies into more complex, sophisticated forms, such as Charlie Parker's "bebop" style of jazz.

4. After charismatic band leaders such as Duke Ellington and Count Basie brought jazz to a larger audience, and jazz continued to evolve into more complicated forms, white audiences began to accept and even to enjoy the new American art form.

5. Many white Americans, who then dictated the tastes of society, were wary of music that was played almost exclusively in black clubs in the poorer sections of cities and towns.

The best order is
   A. 5 4 3 2 1
   B. 2 5 3 4 1
   C. 4 5 3 1 2
   D. 1 2 4 3 5

Question 4

1. Then, hanging in a windless place, the magnetized end of the needle would always point to the south.

2. The needle could then be balanced on the rim of a cup, or the edge of a fingernail, but this balancing act was hard to maintain, and the needle often fell off.

3. Other needles would point to the north, and it was important for any traveler finding his way with a compass to remember which kind of magnetized needle he was carrying.

4. To make some of the earliest compasses in recorded history, ancient Chinese "magicians" would rub a needle with a piece of magnetized iron called a lodestone.

5. A more effective method of keeping the needle free to swing with its magnetic pull was to attach a strand of silk to the center of the needle with a tiny piece of wax.

The best order is
   A. 4 2 5 1 3
   B. 4 3 5 2 1
   C. 4 5 2 1 3
   D. 4 1 3 5 2

Question 5

1. The now-famous first mate of the HMS Bounty, Fletcher Christian, founded one of the world's most peculiar civilizations in 1790.

2. The men knew they had just committed a crime for which they could be hanged, so they set sail for Pitcairn, a remote, abandoned island in the far eastern region of the Polynesian archipelago, accompanied by twelve Polynesian women and six men.

3. In a mutiny that has become legendary, Christian and the others forced Captain Bligh into a lifeboat and set him adrift off the coast of Tonga in April of 1789.

4. In early 1790, the Bounty landed at Pitcairn Island, where the men lived out the rest of their lives and founded an isolated community which to this day includes direct descendants of Christian and the other crewmen.

5. The Bounty, commanded by Captain William Bligh, was in the middle of a global voyage, and Christian and his shipmates had come to the conclusion that Bligh was a reckless madman who would lead them to their deaths unless they took the ship from him.

The best order is
   A. 4 5 3 2 1
   B. 1 3 5 2 4
   C. 1 5 3 2 4
   D. 3 1 5 4 2

Question 6

1. But once the vines had been led to make orchids, the flowers had to be carefully hand-pollinated, because unpollinated orchids usually lasted less than a day, wilting and dropping off the vine before it had even become dark.

2. The Totonac farmers discovered that looping a vine back around once it reached a five-foot height on its host tree would cause the vine to flower.

3. Though they knew how to process the fruit pods and extract vanilla's flavoring agent, the Totonacs also knew that a wild vanilla vine did not produce abundant flowers or fruit.

4. Wild vines climbed along the trunks and canopies of trees, and this constant upward growth diverted most of the vine's energy to making leaves instead of the orchid flowers that, once pollinated, would produce the flavorful pods.

5. Hundreds of years before vanilla became a prized food flavoring in Europe and the Western World, the Totonac Indians of the Mexican Gulf Coast were skilled cultivators of the vanilla vine, whose fruit they literally worshipped as a goddess.

The best order is
A. 2 3 4 1 5
B. 2 4 3 1 5
C. 5 3 4 2 1
D. 3 4 1 2 5

Question 7

1. Once airborne, the spider is at the mercy of the air currents – usually the spider takes a brief journey, traveling close to the ground, but some have been found in air samples collected as high as 10,000 feet, or been reported landing on ships far out at sea.

2. Once a young spider has hatched, it must leave the environment into which it was born as quickly as possible, in order to avoid competing with its hundreds of brothers and sisters for food.

3. The silk rises into warm air currents, and as soon as the pull feels adequate the spider lets go and drifts up into the air, suspended from the silk strand in the same way that a person might parasail.

4. To help young spiders do this, many species have adapted a practice known as "aerial dispersal," or, in common speech, "ballooning."

5. A spider that wants to leave its surroundings quickly will climb to the top of a grass stem or twig, face into the wind, and aim its back end into the air, releasing a long stream of silk from the glands near the tip of its abdomen.

The best order is
A. 5 4 2 3 1
B. 5 2 4 1 3
C. 2 5 4 3 1
D. 2 4 5 3 1

Question 8

1. For about a year, Tycho worked at a castle in Prague with a scientist named Johannes Kepler, but their association was cut short by another argument that drove Kepler out of the castle, to later develop, on his own, the theory of planetary orbits.

2. Tycho found life without a nose embarrassing, so he made a new nose for himself out of silver, which reportedly remained glued to his face for the rest of his life.

3. Tycho Brahe, the 17th-century Danish astronomer, is today more famous for his odd and arrogant personality than for any contribution he has made to our knowledge of the stars and planets.

4. Early in his career, as a student at Rostock University, Tycho got into an argument with the another student about who was the better mathematician, and the two became so angry that the argument turned into a sword fight, during which Tycho's nose was sliced off.

5. Later in his life, Tycho's arrogance may have kept him from playing a part in one of the greatest astronomical discoveries in history: the elliptical orbits of the solar system's planets.

The best order is
    A. 1 4 2 3 5
    B. 4 2 3 5 1
    C. 4 2 1 3 5
    D. 3 4 2 5 1

Question 9

1. The processionaries are so used to this routine that if a person picks up the end of a silk line and brings it back to the origin – creating a closed circle – the caterpillars may travel around and around for days, sometimes starving or freezing, without changing course.

2. Rather than relying on sight or sound, the other caterpillars, who are lined up end-to-end behind the leader, travel to and from their nests by walking on this silk line, and each will reinforce it by laying down its own marking line as it passes over.

3. In order to insure the safety of individuals, the processionary caterpillar nests in a tree with dozens of other caterpillars, and at night, when it is safest, they all leave together in search of food.

4. The processionary caterpillar of the European continent is a perfect illustration of how much some insect species rely on instinct in their daily routines.

5. As they leave their nests, the processionaries form a single-file line behind a leader who spins and lays out a silk line to mark the chosen path.

The best order is
    A. 4 3 5 2 1
    B. 3 5 4 2 1
    C. 3 5 2 1 4
    D. 4 5 3 1 2

Question 10

1. Often, the child is also given a handcrafted walker or push cart, to provide support for its first upright explorations.

2. In traditional Indian families, a child's first steps are celebrated as a ceremonial event, rooted in ancient myth.

3. These carts are often intricately designed to resemble the chariot of Krishna, an important figure in Indian mythology.

4. The sound of these anklet bells is intended to mimic the footsteps of the legendary child Rama, who is celebrated in devotional songs throughout India.

5. When the child's parents see that the child is ready to begin walking, they will fit it with specially designed ankle bracelets, adorned with gently ringing bells.

The best order is
   A. 2 3 4 1 5
   B. 2 5 3 1 4
   C. 5 4 1 3 2
   D. 5 3 2 1 4

Question 11

1. The settlers planted Osage orange all across Middle America, and today long lines and rectangles of Osage orange trees can still be seen on the prairies, running along the former boundaries of farms that no longer exist.

2. After trying sod walls and water-filled ditches with no success, American farmers began to look for a plant that was adaptable to prairie weather, and that could be trimmed into a hedge that was "pig-tight, horse-high, and bull-strong."

3. The tree, so named because it bore a large (but inedible) fruit the size of an orange, was among the sturdiest and hardiest of American trees, and was prized among Native Americans for the strength and flexibility of bows which were made from its wood.

4. The first people to practice agriculture on the American flatlands were faced with an important problem: what would they use to fence their land in a place that was almost entirely without trees or rocks?

5. Finally, an Illinois farmer brought the settlers a tree that was native to the land between the Red and Arkansas rivers, a tree called the Osage orange.

The best order is
   A. 2 1 5 3 4
   B. 1 2 3 4 5
   C. 4 2 5 3 1
   D. 4 2 1 3 5

Question 12

1. After about ten minutes of such spirited and complicated activity, the head dancer is free to make up his or her own movements while maintaining the interest of the New Year's crowd.

2. The dancer will then perform a series of leg kicks, while at the same time operating the lion's mouth with his own hand and moving the ears and eyes by means of a string which is attached to the dancer's own mouth.

3. The most difficult role of this dance belongs to the one who controls the lion's head; this person must lead all the other "parts" of the lion through the choreographed segments of the dance.

4. The head dancer begins with a complex series of steps, alternately stepping forward with the head raised, and then retreating a few steps while lowering the head, a movement that is intended to create the impression that the lion is keeping a watchful eye for anything evil.

5. When performing a traditional Chinese New Year's lion dance, several performers must fit themselves inside a large lion costume and work together to enact different parts of the dance.

The best order is
A. 5 3 4 2 1
B. 3 4 2 5 1
C. 3 1 5 4 2
D. 4 2 3 5 1

Question 13

13._____

1. For many years the shell of the chambered nautilus was treasured in Europe for its beauty and intricacy, but collectors were unaware that they were in possession of the structure that marked a "missing link" in the evolution of marine mollusks.

2. The nautilus, however, evolved a series of enclosed chambers in its shell, and invented a new use for the structure: the shell began to serve as a buoyancy device.

3. Equipped with this new flotation device, the nautilus did not need the single, muscular foot of its predecessors, but instead developed flaps, tentacles, and a gentle form of jet propulsion that transformed it into the first mollusk able to take command of its own destiny and explore a three-dimensional world.

4. By pumping and adjusting air pressure into the chambers, the nautilus could spend the day resting on the bottom, and then rise toward the surface at night in search of food.

5. The nautilus shell looks like a large snail shell, similar to those of its ancestors, who used their shells as protective coverings while they were anchored to the sea floor.

The best order is
A. 5 2 4 1 3
B. 5 1 2 3 4
C. 1 2 5 3 4
D. 1 5 2 4 3

Question 14

1. While France and England battled for control of the region, the Acadiens prospered on the fertile farmland, which was finally secured by England in 1713.

2. Early in the 17th century, settlers from western France founded a colony called Acadie in what is now the Canadian province of Nova Scotia.

3. At this time, English officials feared the presence of spies among the Acadiens who might be loyal to their French homeland, and the Acadiens were deported to spots along the Atlantic and Caribbean shores of America.

4. The French settlers remained on this land, under English rule, for around forty years, until the beginning of the French and Indian War, another conflict between France and England.

5. As the Acadien refugees drifted toward a final home in southern Louisiana, neighbors shortened their name to "'Cadien," and finally "Cajun," the name which the descendants of early Acadiens still call themselves.

The best order is
A. 1 4 2 3 5
B. 2 1 3 5 4
C. 2 1 4 3 5
D. 5 2 3 4 1

Question 15

1. Traditional households in the Eastern and Western regions of Africa serve two meals a day – one at around noon, and the other in the evening.

2. The starch is then used in the way that Americans might use a spoon, to scoop up a portion of the main dish on the person's plate.

3. The reason for the starch's inclusion in every meal has to do with taste as well as nutrition; African food can be very spicy, and the starch is known to cool the burning effect of the main dish.

4. When serving these meals, the main dish is usually served on individual plates, and the starch is served on a communal plate, from which diners break off a piece of bread or scoop rice or fufu in their fingers.

5. The typical meals usually consist of a thick stew or soup as the main course, and an accompanying starch – either bread, rice, or *fufu*, a starchy grain paste similar in consistency to mashed potatoes.

The best order is
A. 5 2 3 4 1
B. 5 1 4 3 2
C. 1 4 5 3 2
D. 1 5 4 2 3

Question 16

1. In the early days of the American Midwest, Indiana settlers sometimes came together to hold an event called an apple peeling, where neighboring settlers gathered at the homestead of a host family to help prepare the hosts' apple crop for cooking, canning, and making apple butter.

2. At the beginning of the event, each peeler sat down in front of a ten- or twenty-gallon stone jar and was given a crock of apples and a paring knife.

3. Once a peeler had finished with a crock, another was placed next to him; if the peeler was an unmarried man, he kept a strict count of the number of apples he had peeled, because the winner was allowed to kiss the girl of his choice.

4. The peeling usually ended by 9:30 in the evening, when the neighbors gathered in the host family's parlor for a dance social.

5. The apples were peeled, cored, and quartered, and then placed into the jar.

The best order is
   A. 1 5 3 4 2
   B. 2 5 3 4 1
   C. 1 2 5 3 4
   D. 2 1 5 4 3

Question 17

1. If your pet turtle is a land turtle and is native to temperate climates, it will stop eating some time in October, which should be your cue to prepare the turtle for hibernation.

2. The box should then be covered with a wire screen, which will protect the turtle from any rodents or predators that might want to take advantage of a motionless and helpless animal.

3. When your turtle hasn't eaten for a while and appears ready to hibernate, it should be moved to its winter quarters, most likely a cellar or garage, where the temperature should range between 40° and 45°F.

4. Instead of feeding the turtle, you should bathe it every day in warm water, to encourage the turtle to empty its intestines in preparation for its long winter sleep.

5. Here the turtle should be placed in a well-ventilated box whose bottom is covered with a moisture-absorbing layer of clay beads, and then filled three-fourths full with almost dry peat moss or wood chips, into which the turtle will burrow and sleep for several months.

The best order is
   A. 1 4 3 5 2
   B. 3 4 2 5 1
   C. 3 2 4 1 5
   D. 4 5 2 3 1

Question 18

1. Once he has reached the nest, the hunter uses two sturdy bamboo poles like huge chopsticks to pull the nest away from the mountainside, into a large basket that will be lowered to people waiting below.

2. The world's largest honeybees colonize the Nepalese mountainsides, building honeycombs as large as a person on sheer rock faces that are often hundreds of feet high.

3. In the remote mountain country of Nepal, a small band of "honey hunters" carry out a tradition so ancient that 10,000 year-old drawings of the practice have been found in the caves of Nepal.

4. To harvest the honey and beeswax from these combs, a honey hunter climbs above the nests, lowers a long bamboo-fiber ladder over the cliff, and then climbs down.

5. Throughout this dangerous practice, the hunter is stung repeatedly, and only the veterans, with skin that has been toughened over the years, are able to return from a hunt without the painful swelling caused by stings.

The best order is
A. 2 4 3 5 1
B. 2 4 1 5 3
C. 5 3 2 4 1
D. 3 2 4 1 5

Question 19

1. After the Romans left Britain, there were relentless attacks on the islands from the barbarian tribes of northern Germany – the Angles, Saxons, and Jutes.

2. As the empire weakened, Roman soldiers withdrew from Britain, leaving behind a country that continued to practice the Christian religion that had been introduced by the Romans.

3. Early Latin writings tell of a Christian warrior named Arturius (Arthur, in English) who led the British citizens to defeat these barbarian invaders, and brought an extended period of peace to the lands of Britain.

4. Long ago, the British Isles were part of the far-flung Roman Empire that extended across most of Europe and into Africa and Asia.

5. The romantic legend of King Arthur and his Knights of the Round Table, one of the most popular and widespread stories of all time, appears to have some foundation in history.

The best order is
A. 5 4 3 2 1
B. 5 4 2 1 3
C. 4 5 2 3 1
D. 4 3 2 1 5

Question 20

1. The cylinder was allowed to cool until it could stand on its own, and then it was cut from the tube and split down the side with a single straight cut.

2. Nineteenth-century glassmakers, who had not yet discovered the glazier's modern techniques for making panes of glass, had to create a method for converting their blown glass into flat sheets.

3. The bubble was then pierced at the end to make a hole that opened up while the glassmaker gently spun it, creating a cylinder of glass.

4. Turned on its side and laid on a conveyor belt, the cylinder was strengthened, or tempered, by being heated again and cooled very slowly, eventually flattening out into a single rectangular piece of glass.

5. To do this, the glassmaker dipped the end of a long tube into melted glass and blew into the other end of the tube, creating an expanding bubble of glass.

The best order is
A. 2 5 3 4 1
B. 2 4 5 3 1
C. 3 5 2 4 1
D. 3 1 4 5 2

Question 21

1. The splints are almost always hidden, but horses are occasionally born whose splinted toes project from the leg on either side, just above the hoof.

2. The second and fourth toes remained, but shrank to thin splints of bone that fused invisibly to the horse's leg bone.

3. Horses are unique among mammals, having evolved feet that each end in what is essentially a single toe, capped by a large, sturdy hoof.

4. Julius Caesar, an emperor of ancient Rome, was said to have owned one of these three-toed horses, and considered it so special that he would not permit anyone else to ride it.

5. Though the horse's earlier ancestors possessed the traditional mammalian set of five toes on each foot, the horse has retained only its third toe; its first and fifth toes disappeared completely as the horse evolved.

The best order is
A. 3 5 2 1 4
B. 5 3 2 4 1
C. 3 2 5 1 4
D. 5 2 3 1 4

Question 22

1. The new building materials – some of which are twenty feet long, and weigh nearly six tons – were transported to Pohnpei on rafts, and were brought into their present position by using hibiscus fiber ropes and leverage to move the stone columns upward along the inclined trunks of coconut palm trees.

2. The ancestors built great fires to heat the stone, and then poured cool seawater on the columns, which caused the stone to contract and split along natural fracture lines.

3. The now-abandoned enclave of Nan Madol, a group of 92 man-made islands off the shore of the Micronesian island of Pohnpei, is estimated to have been built around the year 500 A.D.

4. The islanders say their ancestors quarried stone columns from a nearby island, where large basalt columns were formed by the cooling of molten lava.

5. The structures of Nan Madol are remarkable for the sheer size of some of the stone "logs" or columns that were used to create the walls of the off-shore community, and today anthropologists can only rely on the information of existing local people for clues about how Nan Madol was built.

The best order is
   A. 5 4 3 2 1
   B. 5 3 1 4 2
   C. 3 5 4 2 1
   D. 3 1 4 2 5

Question 23

1. One of the most easily manipulated substances on earth, glass can be made into ceramic tiles that are composed of over 90% air.

2. NASA's space shuttles are the first spacecraft ever designed to leave and re-enter the earth's atmosphere while remaining intact.

3. These ceramic tiles are such effective insulators that when a tile emerges from the oven in which it was fired, it can be held safely in a person's hand by the edges while its interior still glows at a temperature well over 2000°F.

4. Eventually, the engineers were led to a material that is as old as our most ancient civilizations – glass.

5. Because the temperature during atmospheric re-entry is so incredibly hot, it took NASA's engineers some time to find a substance capable of protecting the shuttles.

The best order is
   A. 5 2 1 3 4
   B. 2 5 4 1 3
   C. 2 3 1 4 5
   D. 5 4 3 1 2

Question 24

1. The secret to teaching any parakeet to talk is patience, and the understanding that when a bird "talks," it is simply imitating what it hears, rather than putting ideas into words.

2. You should stay just out of sight of the bird and repeat the phrase you want it to learn, for at least fifteen minutes every morning and evening.

3. It is important to leave the bird without any words of encouragement or farewell; otherwise it might combine stray remarks or phrases, such as "Good night," with the phrase you are trying to teach it.

4. For this reason, to train your bird to imitate your words you should keep it free of any distractions, especially other noises, while you are giving it "lessons."

5. After your repetition, you should quietly leave the bird alone for a while, to think over what it has just heard.

The best order is
A. 1 4 2 5 3
B. 1 2 4 3 5
C. 3 2 1 5 4
D. 3 1 5 4 2

Question 25

1. As a school approaches, fishermen from neighboring communities join their fishing boats together as a fleet, and string their gill nets together to make a huge fence that is held up by cork floats.

2. At a signal from the party leaders, or *nakura*, the family members pound the sides of the boats or beat the water with long poles, creating a sudden and deafening noise.

3. The fishermen work together to drag the trap into a half-circle that may reach 300 yards in diameter, and then the families move their boats to form the other half of the circle around the school of fish.

4. The school of fish flee from the commotion into the awaiting trap, where a final wall of net is thrown over the open end of the half-circle, securing the day's haul.

5. Indonesian people from the area around the Sulu islands live on the sea, in floating villages made of lashed-together or stilted homes, and make much of their living by fishing their home waters for migrating schools of snapper, scad, and other fish.

The best order is
A. 1 5 3 4 2
B. 1 2 4 3 5
C. 5 1 2 3 4
D. 5 1 3 2 4

KEY (CORRECT ANSWERS)

1. D	11. C	21. A
2. D	12. A	22. C
3. B	13. D	23. B
4. A	14. C	24. A
5. C	15. D	25. D
6. C	16. C	
7. D	17. A	
8. D	18. D	
9. A	19. B	
10. B	20. A	

INTERPRETING STATISTICAL DATA
GRAPHS, CHARTS AND TABLES

DIRECTIONS: Each question or incomplete statement is followed by several suggested answers or completions. Select the one that BEST answers the question or completes the statement. *PRINT THE LETTER OF THE CORRECT ANSWER IN THE SPACE AT THE RIGHT.*

TEST 1

Questions 1-5.

DIRECTIONS: Questions 1 through 5 are to be answered SOLELY on the basis of the following chart.

	DUPLICATION JOBS						
JOB. NO.	DATES Submitted	Required	Completed	PROCESS	NO. OF ORIGINALS	NO. OF COPIES OF EACH ORIGINAL	REQUESTING UNIT
324	6/22	6/25	6/25	Xerox	14	25	Research
325	6/25	6/27	6/28	Kodak	10	125	Training
326	6/25	6/25	6/25	Xerox	12	11	Budget
327	6/25	6/27	6/26	Press	17	775	Admin. Div. H
328	6/28	ASAP*	6/25	Press	5	535	Personnel
329	6/26	6/26	6/27	Xerox	15	8	Admin. Div. G

*ASAP - As soon as possible

1. The unit whose job was to be xeroxed but was NOT completed by the date required is
   A. Administrative Division H
   B. Administrative Division G
   C. Research
   D. Training

1.___

2. The job with the LARGEST number of original pages to be   2.___
   xeroxed is job number
      A. 324   B. 326   C. 327   D. 329

3. Jobs were completed AFTER June 26,   for   3.___
      A. Training and Administrative Division G
      B. Training and Administrative Division H
      C. Research and Budget
      D. Administrative Division G *only*

4. Which one of the following units submitted a job which   4.___
   was completed SOONER than required?
      A. Training
      B. Administrative Division H
      C. Personnel
      D. Administrative Division G

5. The jobs which were submitted on different days but were   5.___
   completed on the SAME day and used the SAME process had
   job numbers
      A. 324 and 326   B. 327 and 328
      C. 324, 326, and 328   D. 324, 326, and 329

TEST 2

Questions 1-10.

DIRECTIONS: Questions 1 through 10 are to be answered SOLELY on the basis of the Production Record table shown below for the Information Unit in Agency X for the work week ended Friday, December 6. The table shows, for each employee, the quantity of each type of work performed and the percentage of the work week spent in performing each type of work.

NOTE: Assume that each employee works 7 hours a day and 5 days a week, making a total of 35 hours for the work week.

PRODUCTION RECORD - INFORMATION UNIT IN AGENCY X

(For the work week ended Friday, December 6)

	NUMBER OF			
	Papers Filed	Sheets Proofread	Visitors Received	Envelopes Addressed
Miss Agar	3120	33	178	752
Mr. Brun	1565	59	252	724
Miss Case	2142	62	214	426
Mr. Dale	4259	29	144	1132
Miss Earl	2054	58	212	878
Mr. Farr	1610	69	245	621
Miss Glen	2390	57	230	790
Mr. Hope	3425	32	176	805
Miss Iver	3726	56	148	650
Mr. Joad	3212	55	181	495

	PERCENTAGE OF WORK WEEK SPENT ON				
	Filing Papers	Proof-reading	Receiving Visitors	Addressing Envelopes	Performing Miscellaneous Work
Miss Agar	30%	9%	34%	11%	16%
Mr. Brun	13%	15%	52%	10%	10%
Miss Case	23%	18%	38%	6%	15%
Mr. Dale	50%	7%	17%	16%	10%
Miss Earl	24%	14%	37%	14%	11%
Mr. Farr	16%	19%	48%	8%	9%
Miss Glenn	27%	12%	42%	12%	7%
Mr. Hope	38%	8%	32%	13%	9%
Miss Iver	43%	13%	24%	9%	11%
Mr. Joad	33%	11%	36%	7%	13%

1. For the week, the average amount of time which the employees spent in proofreading was MOST NEARLY _____ hours.
   A. 3.1   B. 3.6   C. 4.4   D. 5.1

      1.___

2. The average number of visitors received daily by an employee was MOST NEARLY
   A. 40   B. 57   C. 198   D. 395

      2.___

3. Of the following employees, the one who addressed envelopes at the FASTEST rate was
   A. Miss Agar B. Mr. Brun C. Miss Case D. Mr. Dale

      3.___

4. Mr. Farr's rate of filing papers was MOST NEARLY _____ pages per minute.
   A. 2   B. 1.7   C. 5   D. 12

      4.___

5. The average number of hours that Mr. Brun spent daily on receiving visitors exceeded the average number of hours that Miss Iver spent daily on the same type of work by MOST NEARLY _____ hours.
   A. 2   B. 3   C. 4   D. 5

      5.___

6. Miss Earl worked at a FASTER rate than Miss Glen in
   A. filing papers   B. proofreading sheets
   C. receiving visitors   D. addressing envelopes

      6.___

7. Mr. Joad's rate of filing papers _____ Miss Iver's rate of filing papers by APPROXIMATELY _____.
   A. was less than; 10%   B. exceeded; 33%
   C. was less than; 16%   D. exceeded; 12%

      7.___

8. Assume that in the following week Miss Case is instructed to increase the percentage of her time spent on filing papers to 35%.
   If she continued to file papers at the same rate as she did for the week ended December 6, the number of additional papers that she filed the following week was MOST NEARLY
   A. 3260   B. 5400   C. 250   D. 1120

      8.___

9. Assume that in the following week Mr. Hope increased his weekly total of envelopes addressed to 1092.
   If he continued to spend the same amount of time on this assignment as he did for the week ended December 6, the increase in his rate of addressing envelopes the following week was MOST NEARLY _____ envelopes per hour.
   A. 15   B. 65   C. 155   D. 240

      9.___

10. Assume that in the following week Miss Agar and Mr. Dale spent 3 and 9 hours less, respectively, on filing papers than they had spent for the week ended December 6, without changing their rates of work.
    The total number of papers filed during the following week by both Miss Agar and Mr. Dale was MOST NEARLY
    A. 4235   B. 4295   C. 4315   D. 4370

      10.___

TEST 3

Questions 1-6.

DIRECTIONS: Questions 1 through 6 are to be answered SOLELY on
the basis of the chart below.

EMPLOYMENT ERRORS

	Allan	Barry	Cary	David
July	5	4	1	7
Aug.	8	3	9	8
Sept.	7	8	7	5
Oct.	3	6	5	3
Nov.	2	4	4	6
Dec.	5	2	8	4

1. The clerk with the HIGHEST number of errors for the   1.___
    6-month period was
    A. Allan   B. Barry   C. Cary   D. David

2. If the number of errors made by Allan in the six months   2.___
    shown represented one-eighth of the total errors made by
    the unit during the entire year, what was the TOTAL
    number of errors made by the unit for the year?
    A. 124   B. 180   C. 240   D. 360

3. The number of errors made by David in November was what   3.___
    fraction of the total errors made in November?
    A. 1/3   B. 1/6   C. 3/8   D. 3/16

4. The average number of errors made per month per clerk was   4.___
    MOST NEARLY
    A. 4   B. 5   C. 6   D. 7

5. Of the total number of errors made during the six-month   5.___
    period, the percentage made in August was MOST NEARLY
    A. 2%   B. 4%   C. 23%   D. 44%

6. If the number of errors in the unit were to decrease in   6.___
    the next six months by 30%, what would be MOST NEARLY the
    total number of errors for the unit for the next six
    months?
    A. 87   B. 94   C. 120   D. 137

———

5

TEST 4

Questions 1-5.

DIRECTIONS: Questions 1 through 5 are to be answered SOLELY on the basis of the data given below. These data show the performance rates of the employees in a particular division for a period of six months.

Employee	Jan.	Feb.	Mar.	April	May	June
A	96	53	64	48	76	72
B	84	58	69	56	67	79
C	73	68	71	54	59	62
D	98	74	79	66	86	74
E	89	78	67	74	75	77

1. According to the above data, the average monthly performance for a worker is MOST NEARLY   1.___
    A. 66   B. 69   C. 72   D. 75

2. According to the above data, the mean monthly performance for the division is MOST NEARLY   2.___
    A. 350   B. 358   C. 387   D. 429

3. According to the above data, the employee who shows the LEAST month-to-month variation in performance is   3.___
    A. A   B. B   C. C   D. D

4. According to the above data, the employee who shows the GREATEST range in performance is   4.___
    A. A   B. B   C. C   D. D

5. According to the above data, the median employee with respect to performance for the six-month period is   5.___
    A. A   B. B   C. C   D. D

TEST 5

Questions 1-5.

DIRECTIONS: Questions 1 through 5 are to be answered SOLELY on the basis of the chart below, which shows the absences in Unit A for the period November 1 through November 15.

ABSENCE RECORD - UNIT A

November 1 - 15

Date:	1	2	3	4	5	6	7	8	9	10	11	12	13	14	15
Employee:															
Ames	X	S	H					X			H			X	X
Bloom	X		H				X	X	S	S	H	S	S		X
Deegan	X	J	H	J	J	J	X	X			H				X
Howard	X		H					X			H			X	X
Jergens	X	M	H	M	M	M		X			H			X	X
Lange	X		H			S	X	X							X
Morton	X						X	X	V	V	H				X
O'Shea	X		H			O		X			H	X		X	X

CODE FOR TYPES OF ABSENCE
X - Saturday or Sunday
H - Legal Holiday
P - Leave without pay
M - Military Leave
J - Jury duty
V - Vacation
S - Sick Leave
O - Other leave of absence

NOTE: If there is no entry against an employee's name under a date, the employee worked on that date.

1. According to the above chart, NO employee in Unit A was absent on 1.___
   A. leave without pay   B. military leave
   C. other leave of absence   D. vacation

2. According to the above chart, all but one of the employees 2.___
   in Unit A were present on the
   A. 3rd   B. 5th   C. 9th   D. 13th

3. According to the above chart, the ONLY employee who worked 3.___
   on a legal holiday when the other employees were absent are
   A. Deegan and Morton   B. Howard and O'Shea
   C. Lange and Morton   D. Morton and O'Shea

4. According to the above chart, the employee who was absent   4.__
   ONLY on a day that was   a Saturday, Sunday, or legal
   holiday was
       A. Bloom   B. Howard   C. Morton   D. O'Shea

5. The employees who had more absences than anyone else are   5.__
       A. Bloom and Deegan
       B. Bloom, Deegan, and Jergens
       C. Deegan and Jergens
       D. Deegan, Jergens, and O'Shea

———

TEST 6

Questions 1-7.

DIRECTIONS: Questions 1 through 7 are to be answered SOLELY on the basis of the time sheet and instructions given below.

	MON.		TUES.		WED.		THURS.		FRI.	
	IN	OUT	IN	OUT	IN	OUT	IN	OUT	IN	OUT
Walker	8:45	5:02	9:20	5:00	9:00	5:02	Annual Lv.		9:04	5:05
Jones	9:01	5:00	9:03	5:02	9:08	5:01	8:55	5:04	9:00	5:00
Rubins	8:49	5:04	Sick Lv.		9:05	5:04	9:03	5:03	9:04	3:30(PB)
Brown	9:00	5:01	8:55	5:03	9:00	5:05	9:04	5:07	9:05	5:03
Roberts	9:30 (PA)	5:08	8:43	5:07	9:05	5:05	9:09	12:30 (PB)	8:58	5:04

The above time sheet indicates the arrival and leaving times of five telephone operators who punched a time clock in a city agency for the week of April 14. The times they arrived at work in the mornings are indicated in the columns labeled *IN* and the times they left work are indicated in the columns labeled *OUT*. The letters (PA) mean prearranged lateness, and the letters (PB) mean personal business. Time lost for these purposes is charged to annual leave.

The operators are scheduled to arrive at 9:00. However, they are not considered late unless they arrive after 9:05. If they prearrange a lateness, they are not considered late. Time lost through lateness is charged to annual leave. A full day's work is eight hours, from 9:00 to 5:00.

1. Which operator worked the entire week WITHOUT using any annual leave or sick leave time? 1.___
    A. Jones
    C. Roberts
    B. Brown
    D. None of the above

2. On which days was NONE of the operators considered late? 2.___
    A. Monday and Wednesday
    C. Wednesday and Thursday
    B. Monday and Friday
    D. Wednesday and Friday

3. Which operator clocked out at a different time each day of the week? 3.___
    A. Roberts   B. Jones   C. Rubins   D. Brown

4. How many of the operators were considered late on Wednesday? 4.___
    A. 0   B. 1   C. 2   C. 3

5. What was the TOTAL number of charged latenesses for the week of April 14? 5.___
    A. 1   B. 3   C. 5   D. 7

9

6. Which day shows the MOST time charged to all types of   6.__
   leave by all the operators?
   A. Monday   B. Tuesday   C. Wednesday   D. Thursday

7. What operators were considered ON TIME all week?   7.__
   A. Jones and Rubins   B. Rubins and Brown
   C. Brown and Roberts   D. Walker and Brown

TEST 7

Questions 1-10.

DIRECTIONS: Questions 1 through 10 are to be answered SOLELY on the
basis of the information and code tables given below.

In accordance with these code tables, each employee in the
department is assigned a code number consisting of ten digits
arranged from left to right in the following order:
  I.   Division in Which Employed
  II. Title of Position
  III. Annual Salary
  IV. Age
  V.   Number of Years Employed in Department

EXAMPLE: A clerk is 21 years old, has been employed in the department
for three years, and is working in the Supply Division at a yearly
salary of $25,000. His code number is 90-115-13-02-2.

DEPARTMENTAL CODE

TABLE I		TABLE II		TABLE III		TABLE IV		TABLE V	
Code No.	Division in Which Employed	Code No.	Title of Position	Code No.	Annual Salary	Code No.	Age	Code No.	No. of Years Employed in Dept.
10	Accounting	115	Clerk	11	$18,000 or less	01	Under 20 yrs.	1	Less than 1 yr.
20	Construction	155	Typist			02	20 to 29 yrs.		
		175	Stenographer	12	$18,001 to $24,000			2	1 to 5 yrs.
30	Engineering					03	30 to 39 yrs.		
40	Information	237	Bookkeeper	13	$24,001 to $30,000			3	6 to 10 yrs.
50	Maintenance					04	40 to 49 yrs.		
60	Personnel	345	Statistician	14	$30,001 to $36,000			4	11 to 15 yrs.
70	Record					05	50 to 59 yrs.		
80	Research	545	Storekeeper	15	$36,001 to $45,000			5	16 to 25 yrs.
90	Supply					06	60 to 69 yrs.		
		633	Draftsman	16	$45,001 to $60,000			6	26 to 35 yrs.
		665	Civil Engineer			07	70 yrs. or over		
				17	$60,001 to $70,000			7	36 yrs. or over
		865	Machinist						
		915	Porter	18	$70,001 or over				

1. A draftsman employed in the Engineering Division at a
    yearly salary of $34,800 is 36 years old and has been
    employed in the department for 9 years.
    He should be coded
        A. 20-633-13-04-3   B. 30-865-13-03-4
        C. 20-665-14-04-4   D. 30-633-14-03-3   1.___

2. A porter employed in the Maintenance Division at a
    yearly salary of $28,800 is 52 years old and has been
    employed in the department for 6 years.
    He should be coded
        A. 50-915-12-03-3   B. 90-545-12-05-3
        C. 50-915-13-05-3   D. 90-545-13-03-3   2.___

3. Richard White, who has been employed in the department
    for 12 years, receives $50,000 a year as a civil engineer
    in the Construction Division. He is 38 years old.
    He should be coded
        A. 20-665-16-03-4   B. 20-665-15-02-1
        C. 20-633-14-04-2   D. 20-865-15-02-5   3.___

4. An 18 year-old clerk appointed to the department six
    months ago is assigned to the Record Division. His
    annual salary is $21,600.
    He should be coded
        A. 70-115-11-01-1   B. 70-115-12-01-1
        C. 70-115-12-02-1   D. 70-155-12-01-1   4.___

5. An employee has been coded 40-155-12-03-3.
    Of the following statements regarding this employee, the
    MOST accurate one is that he is
        A. a clerk who has been employed in the department for
           at least 6 years
        B. a typist who receives an annual salary which does
           not exceed $24,000
        C. under 30 years of age and has been employed in the
           department for at least 11 years
        D. employed in the Supply Division at a salary which
           exceeds $18,000 per annum   5.___

6. Of the following statements regarding an employee who is
    coded 60-175-13-01-2, the LEAST accurate statement is that
    this employee
        A. is a stenographer in the Personnel Division
        B. has been employed in the department for at least one
           year
        C. receives an annual salary which exceeds $24,000
        D. is more than 20 years of age   6.___

7. The following are the names of four employees of the
    department with their code numbers:
        James Black, 80-345-15-03-4
        William White, 30-633-14-03-4
        Sam Green, 80-115-12-02-3
        John Jones, 10-237-13-04-5   7.___

12

If a salary increase is to be given to the employees who have been employed in the department for 11 years or more and who earn less than $36,001 a year, the two of the above employees who will receive a salary increase are
  A. John Jones and William White
  B. James Black and Sam Green
  C. James Black and William White
  D. John Jones and Sam Green

8. Code number 50-865-14-02-6, which has been assigned to a machinist, contains an obvious inconsistency. This inconsistency involves the figures
  A. 50-865   B. 865-14   C. 14-02   D. 02-6

9. Ten employees were awarded merit prizes for outstanding service during the year. Their code numbers were:

    80-345-14-04-4   40-155-12-02-2
    40-155-12-04-4   10-115-12-02-2
    10-115-13-03-2   80-115-13-02-2
    80-175-13-05-5   10-115-13-02-3
    10-115-12-04-3   30-633-14-04-4

Of these outstanding employees, the number who were clerks employed in the Accounting Division at a salary ranging from $24,001 to $30,000 per annum is
  A. 1   B. 2   C. 3   D. 4

10. The MOST accurate of the following statements regarding the ten outstanding employees listed in the previous question is that
  A. fewer than half of the employees were under 40 years of age
  B. there were fewer typists than stenographers
  C. four of the employees were employed in the department 11 years or more
  D. two of the employees in the Research Division receive annual salaries ranging from $30,001 to $36,000

8.___

9.___

10.___

KEY (CORRECT ANSWERS)

TEST 1	TEST 2	TEST 3	TEST 4	TEST 5	TEST 6	TEST 7
1. B	1. C	1. C	1. C	1. A	1. B	1. B
2. D	2. A	2. C	2. B	2. D	2. B	2. C
3. A	3. B	3. C	3. C	3. C	3. A	3. A
4. B	4. C	4. B	4. A	4. B	4. B	4. B
5. A	5. A	5. C	5. B	5. B	5. B	5. B
	6. C	6. A			6. D	6. D
	7. D				7. B	7. A
	8. D					8. D
	9. B					9. B
	10. B					10. C

BASIC FUNDAMENTALS OF LIBRARY SCIENCE

CONTENTS

BASIC FUNDAMENTALS OF LIBRARY SCIENCE

The problem of classifying all human knowledge has produced a branch of learning called "library science." A lasting contribution to a simple and understandable method of locating a book on any topic was designed by Melvil Dewey in 1876. His plan divided all knowledge into ten large classes and then dubdivided each class according to related groups.

DEWEY DECIMAL SYSTEM

1. Subject Classification
   The Dewey Decimal Classification System is the accepted and most widely used subject classification system in libraries throughout the world.
2. Classification by Three (3) Groups
   There are three groups of classification in the system. A basic group of ten (10) classifications arranges all knowledge as represented by books within groups by classifications numbered 000-900.
   The second group is the "100 division"; each group of the basic "10 divisions" is again divided into 9 sub-sctions allowing for more detailed and specialized subjects not identified in the 10 basic divisions.
3. There is a third, still further specialized "One thousand" group where each of the "100" classifications are further divided by decimalized, more specified, subject classifications. The "1,000" group is mainly used by highly specialized scientific and much diversified libraries.
   These are the subject classes of the Dewey System:

000-099	General works (included bibliography, encyclopedias, collections, periodicals, newspapers, etc.)
100-199	Philosophy (includes psychology, logic, ethics, conduct, etc.)
200-299	Religion (includes mythology, natural theology, Bible, church history, etc.)
300-399	Social Science (includes economics, government, law, education, commerce, etc.)
400-499	Language (includes dictionaries, grammars, philology, etc.)
500-599	Science (includes mathematics, chemistry, physics, astronomy, geology, etc.)
600-699	Useful Arts (includes agriculture, engineering, aviation, medicine, manufactures, etc.)
700-799	Fine Arts (includes sculpture, painting, music, photography, gardening, etc.)
800-899	Literature (includes poetry, plays, orations, etc.)
900-999	History (includes geoegraphy, travel, biography, ancient and modern history, etc.)

PREPARING TO USE THE LIBRARY

Your ability to use the library and its resources is an important factor in determining your success. Skill and efficiency in finding the library materials you need for assignments and research papers will increase the amount of time you have to devote to reading or organizing information.
These are some of the preparations you can make now.

1. Develop skill in using your local library. You can increase your familiarity with the card catalog and the periodical indexes, such as the *Readers' Guide to Periodical Literature,* in any library.
2. Take the *Test in Library Science* to see how you can improve your knowledge of the library.

3. Read in such books as *Books, Libraries and You* by Jessie Edna Boyd, *The Library Key* by Margaret G. Cook, and *Making Books Work, a Guide to the Use of Libraries* by Jennie Maas Flexner.

You can find other titles by looking under the subject heading LIBRARIES AND READERS in the card catalog of your library.

THREE TYPES OF BOOK CARDS

Here are the three general types of cards which are used to represent a book in the main catalog.

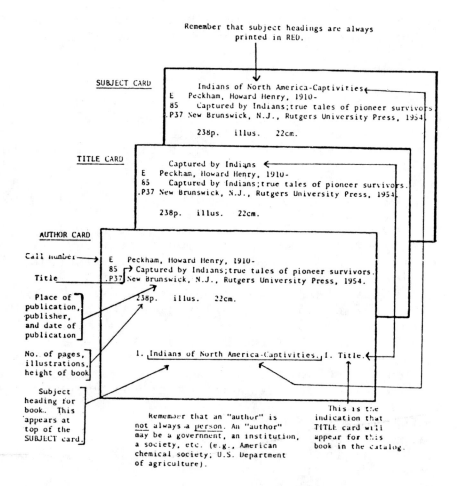

Remember that subject headings are always printed in RED.

SUBJECT CARD

Indians of North America-Captivities
E Peckham, Howard Henry, 1910-
85   Captured by Indians; true tales of pioneer survivors.
.P37 New Brunswick, N.J., Rutgers University Press, 1954.

238p.   illus.   22cm.

TITLE CARD

Captured by Indians
E Peckham, Howard Henry, 1910-
85   Captured by Indians; true tales of pioneer survivors.
.P37 New Brunswick, N.J., Rutgers University Press, 1954.

238p.   illus.   22cm.

AUTHOR CARD

Call number →
Title
Place of publication, publisher, and date of publication
No. of pages, illustrations, height of book
Subject heading for book. This appears at top of the SUBJECT card.

E Peckham, Howard Henry, 1910-
85   Captured by Indians; true tales of pioneer survivors.
.P37 New Brunswick, N.J., Rutgers University Press, 1954.

238p.   illus.   22cm.

1. Indians of North America-Captivities.   I. Title.

Remember that an "author" is not always a person. An "author" may be a government, an institution, a society, etc. (e.g., American chemical society; U.S. Department of agriculture).

This is the indication that TITLE card will appear for this book in the catalog.

CARD CATALOG

The Card Catalog lists all books in the library by author. The majority of books also have title and subject cards.

Author card

If the author is known, look in the catalog under the author's name. The "author" for some works may be a society, an institution, or a government department.

Title card

Books with distinctive titles, anonymous works and periodicals will have a title card.

Subject card

To find books on a specific subject, look in the catalog under that subject heading. (Subject headings are printed in red on the Catalog Card.)

<u>Call number</u>

    The letters and numbers in the upper left-hand corner of the Catalog Card are the book's call number. Copy this call number accurately, for it will determine the shelf location of the book. The word "Reference" marked in red in the upper right-hand corner of the catalog card indicates that the item is shelved in the Reference Section, and "Periodical "marked in yellow on the Catalog Card indicates that the item is shelved in the Periodicals Section.

PERIODICALS

    All magazines are arranged in alphabetical order by title.

PERIODICALS FILE

    To determine whether the Library has a specific magazine, consult the Periodicals File. Check the title of the magazine needed, and note that there are two cards for each title.

    The bottom card lists the current issues available. The top card lists back bound volumes.

    Those marked "Ask at Ref.Desk" may be obtained from the Reference Librarian.

PERIODICAL INDEXES

    Material in magazines is more up-to-date than books and is a valuable source of information. To find articles on a chosen subject, use the periodical indexes.

    The Readers' Guide to Periodical Literature is the most familiar of these indexes. In the front of each volume is a list of the periodicals indexed and a key to abbreviations. Similar aids appear in the front of other periodical indexes.

Sample entry: WEASELS
             WONDERFUL WHITE WEASEL. R.Beck. il OUTDOOR LIFE
             135:48-9+ Ja '65

Explanation : An illustrated article on the subject WEASELS entitled
           WONDERFUL WHITE WEASEL, by R.Beck, will be found in
           volume 135 of OUTDOOR LIFE, pages 48-9 (continued on later pages of the same issue), the January 1965 number.

Major libraries subscribe to the following indexes:

<u>Art Index</u>

<u>Biography Index</u>

<u>Book Review Index</u>

<u>British Humanities Index</u>

<u>Essay and General Literature Index</u>
    This is helpful for locating criticism of works of literature.

<u>An Index to Book Reviews in the Humanities</u>

<u>International Index</u> ceased publications June, 1965 and continued
    as <u>Social Science and Humanities Index</u>

<u>The Music Index</u>

<u>The New York Times Index</u>

<u>Nineteenth Century Readers' Guide</u>

<u>Poole's Index</u>

<u>Poverty and Human Resources Abstracts</u>

<u>Psychological Abstracts</u>

<u>Public Affairs Information Service, Bulletin of the (PAIS)</u> is a subject index to current books, pamphlets, periodical articles, government documents, and other library materials in economics and public affairs.

<u>Readers' Guide to Periodical Literature</u>

<u>Social Science and Humanities Index</u> a continuation of the <u>International Index</u>

<u>Sociological Abstracts</u>

TEST IN LIBRARY SCIENCE

Do you have the basic skills for using a library efficiently? You should be able to answer AT LEAST 33 of the following questions correctly. *CHECK YOUR ANSWERS BY TURNING TO THE ANSWER KEY AT THE BACK OF THIS SECTION.*

I. USING A CARD CATALOG

Questions 1-9.

DIRECTIONS: An author card (or "main entry" card) is shown below. Identify each item on the card by selecting the CORRECT letters for them. *PRINT THE LETTER OF THE CORRECT ANSWER IN THE SPACE AT THE RIGHT.*

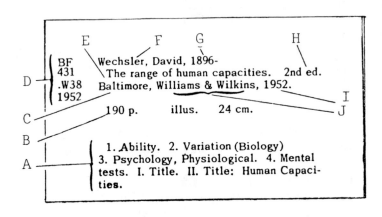

Sample Answer:

0. <u>F</u>

1. Date book was published.   1. ...
2. Number of pages in book.   2. ...
3. Title.   3. ...
4. Place of publication.   4. ...
5. Call number.   5. ...
6. Year author was born,   6. ...
7. Edition.   7. ...
8. Publisher.   8. ...
9. Other headings under which cards for this book may be   9. ...
   found.

Questions 10-13.

DIRECTIONS: Select the letter preceding the word or phrase which completes each of the following statements correctly.

10. The library's title card for the book THE LATE GEORGE AP-   10. ...
    LEY can be found by looking in the card catalog under
        A. Apley,George   B. The   C. Late   D. George   E. Apley

11. A catalog card for a book by John F. Kennedy would be   11. ...
    found in the drawer labelled
        A. JEFFERSON-JOHNSON,ROY
        B. PRESCOTT-PRICELESS
        C. KIERNAN-KLAY
        D. U.S.PRESIDENT-U.S.SOCIAL SECURITY
        E. KENNEBEC-KIERKEGAARD

4

12. The title cards for these three periodicals would be found 12. ...
    in the card catalog arranged in which of the following orders:
    A. NEW YORKER, NEWSWEEK, NEW YORK TIMES MAGAZINE
    B. NEWSWEEK, NEW YORKER, NEW YORK TIMES MAGAZINE
    C. NEW YORK TIMES MAGAZINE, NEW YORKER, NEWSWEEK
    D. NEW YORKER, NEW YORK TIMES MAGAZINE, NEWSWEEK
    E. NEWSWEEK, NEW YORK TIMES MAGAZINE, NEW YORKER

13. A card for a copy of the U.N. Charter would be found in the 13. ...
    catalog drawer marked
    A. TWENTIETH-UNAMUNO
    B. UNITED MINE WORKERS-UNITED SHOE MACHINERY
    C. U.S. BUREAU-U.S. CONGRESS
    D. U.S. SOCIAL POLICY-UNIVERSITAS
    E. CHANCEL-CIARDI

II. UNDERSTANDING ENTRIES IN A PERIODICAL INDEX
    Questions 14-25.
    DIRECTIONS: The following items are excerpts from THE READERS'
                GUIDE TO PERIODICAL LITERATURE. Identify each lettered
                section of the entries by placing the correct letters
                in the spaces. (There are more letters than spaces, so
                some of the letters will not be used.)

A____UNITED NATIONS
    Ambassador Goldberg holds news conference at
    New York; transcript of conference,
B _____July 28, 1965; with questions and answers.
    A. J. Goldberg. Dept. State Bul 53:272+
C____ Ag 16 '65
    U.N. out of its teens. I.D. Talmadge. il Sr Schol
E ____ 87:16-17+ S 16 '65
D ____ Whatever became of the United Nations?
    America 113:235 S 4 '65
                F   R
                        Charter
    Up-dating the pre-atomic United Nations; address,
    June 20, 1965. C.P. Romulo. Vital Speeches
    31:658-61 Ag 15 '65; Excerpts. Sat R 48:34-5+
    Jl 24 '65
            N

H _____Security Council
    Security Council urged to respond to
    challenge in southeast Asia; letter,
M __July 30, 1965. A. J. Goldberg. Dept
    State Bul 53:278-80+ Ag 16, '65
        L   •I   J   K

14. Title of magazine containing a transcript of a news con- 14. ...
    conference held by U.N. Ambassador Arthur Goldberg.
15. Magazine in which the full text of C.P. Romulo's address 15. ...
    on the U.N. appears.
16. Author of an article titled U.N. OUT OF ITS TEENS.   16. ...
17. Date on which Ambassador Goldberg wrote a letter urging   17. ...
    the Security Council to respond to the challenge of south-
    east Asia.
18. Title of an article for which no author is listed.   18. ...
19. Date of the SATURDAY REVIEW issue which contains excerpts 19. ...
    of a speech called "Up-Dating the Pre-Atomic United Nations."
20. Pages in the DEPARTMENT OF STATE BULLETIN on which Am-   20. ...
    bassador Goldberg's letter appears.
21. Symbol indicating that the letter is continued on a la-   21. ...
    ter page.
22. Volume number of the magazine in which the article by   22. ...
    I.D. Talmadge is printed.
23. Symbols meaning September 16, 1965.   23. ...

24. The general subject heading under which all five articles   24. ...
    are listed.
25. A subject heading subdivision.   25. ...
Questions 26-27.
DIRECTIONS: Select the letter preceding the phrase which completes
            each of the following statements correctly.
26. To determine whether or not the library has THE MAGAZINE OF 26. ...
    AMERICAN HISTORY, check in
        A. the list of magazine titles in the front of THE REA-
           DERS' GUIDE TO PERIODICAL LITERATURE
        B. the library's card catalog
        C. Ulrich's GUIDE TO PERIODICALS
        D. SATURDAY REVIEW
        E. THE LIBRARY JOURNAL
27. THE READERS' GUIDE is a good place to look for material on 27. ...
    the Job Corps because it
        A. indexes only the best books and magazines in each field
        B. is a guide to articles on many subjects appearing in
           all of the library's periodicals
        C. indexes recent discussions on the subject in many maga-
           zines
        D. specializes in official government information
        E. does all of the above
III. IDENTIFYING LIBRARY TERMS
     Questions 28-32.
     DIRECTIONS: Match the correct definitions with these terms
                 by placing the correct letters in the blanks.
                 (Some of the letters will not be used.)

28. Bibliography   A. Word or phrase printed in   28. ...
29. Anthology   red at the top of a cata-   29. ...
30. Index   log to indicate the major   30. ...
31. Abstract   topic of the book   31. ...
32. Subject heading   B. Brief written summary of   32. ...
                             the major ideas presented
                             in an article or book
                          C. List of books and/or arti-
                             cles on one subject or
                             by one author
                          D. Collection of selections from
                             the writings of one or sever-
                             al authors
                          E. Written account of a person's
                             life
                          F. Alphabetical list of subjects
                             with the pages on which they
                             are to be found in a book or
                             periodical
                          G. Subordinate, usually explanatory
                             title, additional to the main
                             title and usually printed be-
                             low it

IV. FINDING A BOOK BY ITS CALL NUMBER
   Questions 33-38.
   DIRECTIONS: The Library of Congress classification system call num-
              bers shown below are arranged in order,just as the books
              bearing those call numbers would be arranged on the
              shelves. To show where other call numbers would be lo-
              cated,select the letter of the CORRECT ANSWER.

A.	B.	C.	D.	E.	F.	G.	H.	I.	J.	K.
PS	PS	PS	PS	PS	PS	PS	PS	PS	PS	PS
201	201	208	351	351	3513	3515	3515.3	3526	3526.17	3526.37
.L67	.M44	.B87	.D7	.D77	.A2	.D72	A66	.N21	P2	A10
1961		1944								

L.	M.	N.
PS	PS	PT
3526.37	3526.37	1
C20	C37	.R2

33. A book with the call number PS   would be shelved   33. ...
                                  201
                                  .L67
    A. Before A   B. Between A & B   C. Between B & C
    D. Between C & D   E. Between D & E
34, A book with the call number PS   would be shelved   34. ...
                                  208
                                  .B87
                                  1944a
    A. Between A & B B. Between C & D   C. Between B & C
    D. Between C & D E. Between D & E
35. A book with the call number PS   would be shelved   35. ...
                                  351
                                  .D8
    A. Between C & D B. Between D & E   C. Between E & F
    D. Between F & G E. Between G & H
36. A book with the call number PS   would be shelved   36. ...
                                  3526.3
                                  M53
    A. Between L & M B. Between J & K   C. Between K & L
    D. Between M & O E. Between O & P
37. A book with the call number PS   would be shelved   37. ...
                                  3526.37
                                  C205
    A. Between L & M B. Between N & O   C. Between M & N
    D. Between O & P E. Between P & Q
38. A book with the call number PS   would be shelved   38. ...
                                  3526.37
                                  C3
    A. Between M & N B. Between L & M   C. Between N & O
    D. Between O & P D. Between P & Q

V. General
   Questions 39-40.
   DIRECTIONS: Each question or incomplete statement is followed by
               several suggested answers or completions. Select the
               one that BEST answers the question or completes the
               statement. *PRINT THE LETTER OF THE CORRECT ANSWER IN
               THE SPACE AT THE RIGHT.*

39. When it is finished (in 610 volumes), the _____ 39. ..
    will be the MOST monumental national bibliography in the
    world.
        A. UNION LIST OF SERIALS IN LIBRARIES OF THE UNITED
           STATES AND CANADA
        B. UNITED STATES CATALOG
        C. READERS' GUIDE TO PERIODICAL LITERATURE
        D. NATIONAL UNION CATALOG

40. For those who wish to investigate the publishing com-   40. ..
    panies and the people who control them, to locate the
    date a company was founded, who owned it, when it changed
    hands, what firm succeeded it, and other information of a
    similar nature, the periodical _____ is clearly
    invaluable.
        A. PUBLISHERS' TRADE LIST ANNUAL (PTLA)
        B. CUMULATIVE BOOK INDEX
        C. AMERICAN BOOKTRADE DIRECTORY
        D. PUBLISHERS WEEKLY

—

KEY (CORRECT ANSWERS)

1. I   2. B   3. E   4. C   5. D   6. G   7. H   8. J   9. A
10. C - The first word of the title which is not an article.
11. E - Every book in the library is listed in the card catalog under
        the author's name. (Warning: The "author" may be a society, a
        university, or some other institution.)
12. C - A title is alphabetized word-by-word; therefore,"New" comes
        before "Newsweek," "New York" before "New Yorker."
13. B - The United Nations,not an individual,is the author of this work
14. T   16. Q   18. D   20. J   22. E   24. A   26. B   28. C   30. F   32. A
15. O   17. M   19. N   21. K   23. R   25. P/H   27. C   29. D   31. B
33. A - When two call numbers are identical except that one has a year
        or some other figure added at its end, the shorter call numbers
        comes first.
34. B
35. C - The numbers which follow a. are regarded as decimals; therefore
        .D77 precedes .D8.
36. B - 3526.3 precedes 3526.37
37. A - .C20 precedes .C205
38. B - .C3 precedes .C37
    (Read the call number line-by-line, and put a J before a P, before
     PB, etc. Put a lower number before a greater one.)
39. D
40. D

—

ANSWER SHEET

ST NO. _____ PART _____ TITLE OF POSITION _____
(AS GIVEN IN EXAMINATION ANNOUNCEMENT - INCLUDE OPTION, IF ANY)

ACE OF EXAMINATION _____ DATE ____ _____
(CITY OR TOWN)   (STATE)

RATING

USE THE SPECIAL PENCIL.   MAKE GLOSSY BLACK MARKS.

	A	B	C	D	E		A	B	C	D	E		A	B	C	D	E		A	B	C	D	E		A	B	C	D	E
1						26						51						76						101					
2						27						52						77						102					
3						28						53						78						103					
4						29						54						79						104					
5						30						55						80						105					
6						31						56						81						106					
7						32						57						82						107					
8						33						58						83						108					
9						34						59						84						109					
10						35						60						85						110					

Make only ONE mark for each answer.   Additional and stray marks may be
counted as mistakes.   In making corrections, erase errors COMPLETELY.

	A	B	C	D	E		A	B	C	D	E		A	B	C	D	E		A	B	C	D	E		A	B	C	D	E
11						36						61						86						111					
12						37						62						87						112					
13						38						63						88						113					
14						39						64						89						114					
15						40						65						90						115					
16						41						66						91						116					
17						42						67						92						117					
18						43						68						93						118					
19						44						69						94						119					
20						45						70						95						120					
21						46						71						96						121					
22						47						72						97						122					
23						48						73						98						123					
24						49						74						99						124					
25						50						75						100						125					

ANSWER SHEET

TEST NO. ____________ PART ______ TITLE OF POSITION ______________________________
(AS GIVEN IN EXAMINATION ANNOUNCEMENT - INCLUDE OPTION, IF ANY)

PLACE OF EXAMINATION ______________________________ (CITY OR TOWN) ______________ (STATE) DATE ______________

RATING

USE THE SPECIAL PENCIL. MAKE GLOSSY BLACK MARKS.

1 A B C D E	26 A B C D E	51 A B C D E	76 A B C D E	101 A B C D E
2 A B C D E	27 A B C D E	52 A B C D E	77 A B C D E	102 A B C D E
3 A B C D E	28 A B C D E	53 A B C D E	78 A B C D E	103 A B C D E
4 A B C D E	29 A B C D E	54 A B C D E	79 A B C D E	104 A B C D E
5 A B C D E	30 A B C D E	55 A B C D E	80 A B C D E	105 A B C D E
6 A B C D E	31 A B C D E	56 A B C D E	81 A B C D E	106 A B C D E
7 A B C D E	32 A B C D E	57 A B C D E	82 A B C D E	107 A B C D E
8 A B C D E	33 A B C D E	58 A B C D E	83 A B C D E	108 A B C D E
9 A B C D E	34 A B C D E	59 A B C D E	84 A B C D E	109 A B C D E
10 A B C D E	35 A B C D E	60 A B C D E	85 A B C D E	110 A B C D E

Make only ONE mark for each answer. Additional and stray marks may be counted as mistakes. In making corrections, erase errors COMPLETELY.

11 A B C D E	36 A B C D E	61 A B C D E	86 A B C D E	111 A B C D E
12 A B C D E	37 A B C D E	62 A B C D E	87 A B C D E	112 A B C D E
13 A B C D E	38 A B C D E	63 A B C D E	88 A B C D E	113 A B C D E
14 A B C D E	39 A B C D E	64 A B C D E	89 A B C D E	114 A B C D E
15 A B C D E	40 A B C D E	65 A B C D E	90 A B C D E	115 A B C D E
16 A B C D E	41 A B C D E	66 A B C D E	91 A B C D E	116 A B C D E
17 A B C D E	42 A B C D E	67 A B C D E	92 A B C D E	117 A B C D E
18 A B C D E	43 A B C D E	68 A B C D E	93 A B C D E	118 A B C D E
19 A B C D E	44 A B C D E	69 A B C D E	94 A B C D E	119 A B C D E
20 A B C D E	45 A B C D E	70 A B C D E	95 A B C D E	120 A B C D E
21 A B C D E	46 A B C D E	71 A B C D E	96 A B C D E	121 A B C D E
22 A B C D E	47 A B C D E	72 A B C D E	97 A B C D E	122 A B C D E
23 A B C D E	48 A B C D E	73 A B C D E	98 A B C D E	123 A B C D E
24 A B C D E	49 A B C D E	74 A B C D E	99 A B C D E	124 A B C D E
25 A B C D E	50 A B C D E	75 A B C D E	100 A B C D E	125 A B C D E